RONALD KNOX

RETREAT IN SLOW MOTION

SHEED AND WARD
LONDON AND NEW YORK

FIRST PUBLISHED IN GREAT BRITAIN 1961
SHEED AND WARD LTD
33 MAIDEN LANE
LONDON W.C.2

NIHIL OBSTAT
    GALL HIGGINS, O.F.M.CAP.
    CENSOR LIBRORUM

IMPRIMATUR
    ✠ FRANCIS CARDINAL SPELLMAN
    ARCHBISHOP OF NEW YORK
    MAY 10, 1960

The Nihil Obstat and Imprimatur are official declarations that a book or pamphlet is free of doctrinal or moral error. No implication is contained therein that those who have granted the Nihil Obstat and Imprimatur agree with the contents, opinions or statements expressed.

Made and printed by offset in Great Britain by
William Clowes and Sons, Limited, London and Beccles

Contents

Contents

Editorial Note

MGR. KNOX often gave what was in effect the same meditation to different groups, changing groups, changing phrases, adding or omitting ideas. For this book, as for the three Retreat books listed below, he handed me a mass of typescripts, with a general instruction to make them into a Retreat-to-be-read. Where there were two or more conferences on the same theme, he left the work of conflation to me.

F. J. SHEED

Already published:

A Retreat for Priests
A Retreat for Lay People, with a Preface by the author.
The Priestly Life, published posthumously.

Introduction

A SMALL girl I know had her first experience, some time ago, of hearing a sermon. She had been to Mass before, and that seemed reasonable enough; but she had always been in domestic chapels where the priest kept his back turned to the congregation and got on with his job. And when, one Sunday, a priest came along who turned round and began preaching, it worried her; she asked, in a very loud voice, "Mummy, who's he talking to?" Well, of course she was quite right. A man who gets up and lets off a number of remarks in the air, with the room full of people who may or may not be listening, always looks, and quite often is, foolish. But if you are echoing the small girl's question, and want to know who it is that I am talking to, I have my answer ready. I am talking to you. Not to you in the plural. I am talking to one particular soul, you in the singular.

So please don't think of me as if I were sitting at a microphone, broadcasting, and you couldn't find the right handle for turning the thing off. Think of me as if I had just got your number on the telephone, and were putting through a personal call to you; to you in the singular. You know how idiotic people sometimes start a telephone conversation with the remark, "Hullo, is that you?"—as if it could possibly be anyone else. That question, commonly so idiotic, I want to ask now, because for our particular purposes it has a

meaning; *is that you?* I mean, are we really going to talk
honestly to one another, you and I, or are you going to put
up some sort of barrage all the time, because I'm a priest,
and you know the sort of things priests always say, and you
don't want to listen to it?

I *What a Retreat Is For*

WHAT *is* the point of a retreat? I should put it like this—
that God means to do something in and to your soul. It may
be something quite little; almost certainly it will seem quite
little. But then, of course, that little may be the thin end of
a wedge. He wants to do a sort of tidying-up, a sort of
spring-cleaning in your life; perhaps he will open your eyes
to some fault, perhaps he will begin to wean you away from
some bad habit, some dangerous friendship, perhaps he will
give you a glimpse of some way (you hadn't thought about
it hitherto) in which, later on, he means you to serve him.
It may be that something I say will be the signal, don't let
us put it any higher than that, just the signal, for some new
train of thought to start rumbling through your brain. Probably you won't be conscious that the thing is happening.

I think you will probably be disposed to agree with me
when I say that there is nothing so uninteresting as other
people's conversation in railway trains. Occasionally such
people will say something exquisitely funny without meaning
it, which you treasure up to repeat to your friends afterwards, but for the most part it is so inane that you wonder
they don't shut up altogether. I did, though, not very long
ago, hear a story in that way which seemed to me a good
story, and I treasured it up for use; particularly for use on
occasions like this. It is a very simple story—there was a

porter going round hitting the wheels of the carriages with a hammer, as you see them doing now and again in the course of a long run, at Carlisle or at York or somewhere like that. And a passenger went up and said, "How long have you been doing that for?" And the porter said, "Twenty years, Sir." And the passenger said, "What do you do it for?" And the porter said, "Dunno, Sir." He was probably sick of being asked.

Most of us could give that answer to a good many questions, at least while we're at school. We are prepared to go on and on doing a thing, however laborious it may be in itself, as long as we are not expected to take the trouble to find out what it is for. When I was at school, for example, I used to have to do a lot of things called quadratic equations; I don't know whether they have been abolished yet or not. I must have spent weeks of my life over quadratic equations, but I've never met one in real life, and I am still wondering what I did quadratic equations for. Probably they were very good for one in some way. Well, most of you are doing things like that, Latin exercises and what not; and the only question you are never encouraged to ask is *why*. The reason why you are not encouraged to ask why is because it holds up the business of the class if you do; and a grave suspicion arises that you asked the question in order to hold up the business of the class. So you are told to shut up.

In the nursery, one asks Why much too often. At school, the habit is bred out of you, and you ask Why, perhaps, too little. Or at least there is one department of life in which the habit of not asking Why can be dangerous; and that is, where your religion is concerned. School is such a dreadful place for falling into ruts of habit; and it's possible to fall into ruts of good habit as well as bad. You can get into the habit of saying your prayers, going to confession, going to Communion, and so on, all at regular intervals, *merely* by force of habit—and that's a pity. If you ask yourself how often you go to Communion in the holidays, you'll see what I mean. And it's possible to make the same mistake even with things that only come at long intervals, like going into retreat. Many of you, if I asked how many years of your life you'd spent going into retreat twice a year, would have to say four, some of you even five. And if I asked you what you did it for, you would probably have to say, like the porter, "I dunno." Well, of course, that's absurd; there must be some reason for going into retreat. Let's go back to that porter, if you're not tired of him by now.

When I was in the nursery and fond of asking questions, I naturally asked what the man was doing when he came and tapped the wheels. And what they told me was that he was testing the wheels after so many miles of run, to make sure that they weren't cracked. If they were cracked, they would make a different sort of noise, and then it would be great fun, because we should all have to get out and be moved into another carriage. I don't know whether they were giving the true explanation, or just telling me any story that came into their heads by way of making me shut up; I never heard one of the wheels make a cracked noise, though of course I used to listen very carefully. But if their account was the true one, I think it makes rather a good parable of our lives, and of the place which a retreat is meant to have in our lives.

Our lives run on as if on wheels, and the years slip past us without our noticing, like the unimportant stations on a big line of railway. All the time we are taking wear out of ourselves, as the train is taking wear out of its wheels on a long journey. You get accustomed to the motion and the noise; you cease to notice it, and in the end it almost puts you to sleep. But it's frightening to remember how the wheels are buzzing round all the time, and the friction they have to endure and the weight they have to carry. What more likely, you would think, than that some tiny flaw should form itself in the wheel, while nobody is thinking about it? It's a good thing that just now and again, at Carlisle maybe or at York, the train should come to a standstill, and a man should go round with a hammer to make sure there's nothing wrong. Just in the same way, the even tenor of our lives encourages us to go on, go on, go on, without thinking, without wondering what is happening to us. Mass and breakfast and work and luncheon and games and tea and work and supper and bed and Mass and breakfast and work and luncheon and games and tea and work and supper and Mass and breakfast and so on and so on and then, suddenly, there's a grinding of brakes and a slowing down of wheels and porters begin to shout. That's when we go into retreat.

And the retreat father's job, as I see it, is to go round like the porter with the hammer, giving a tap here and a tap there, not so much by way of putting right things that have gone wrong, as by way of making certain that things *haven't* gone wrong, making certain that everything rings true in *your* life and *your* life and *your* life, that have been hurrying along so quickly and so thoughtlessly since last year. Your faith, for example—there's not likely to be anything wrong with that, still, it's just worth tapping it to make sure. You learned your Catechism when you were small, and you've been doing Christian doctrine at school, and it's not likely that you have been taught any heresies yet; but it's possible, isn't it, to get things mixed up that you've heard in class, to get hold of the wrong end of the stick and come out with some whopping great heresy at the tea-table. Well, there's no need for me to remind you how important a right faith is to Catholics. Get wrong on one point, if it's a point of any importance, and it throws your whole mind out of the straight; it's as if you have one wheel of a railway-carriage oval instead of round, and that would be a very uncomfortable carriage to travel in, wouldn't it?

Well, in the course of these retreat conferences I shall be talking a certain amount of theology by the way, though only of the simplest kind; about what God is and what your soul is and what the Incarnation means and what the Passion means and so on. If you hear me say anything that sounds odd, that doesn't seem exactly like what you've always been brought up to believe, don't take it lying down. Say to yourself, Either this man is talking through his hat, or I've got the thing wrong somewhere. Go to one of the teachers and talk it over. Perhaps I'm wrong, perhaps you are; it would be a dreadful thing, wouldn't it, if you or I were going about quite misinformed about what the Catholic Church teaches? Don't let some tiny sore of heresy fester and rankle in your mind; bring it out to the light and clear it up by arguing about it, or it will fester and rankle more and more, and give you trouble later on.

I know what I am talking about when I say that there are tragedies, not seldom, in Christian lives which could have been avoided if people had taken a little more trouble and shewn a little more frankness over the things that puzzled them about the Faith, while they were still at school. When I was a schoolmaster, I used sometimes to start going through the lesson, translating, say, a piece of Latin myself, and putting in all the mistakes I could think of; and when the class had sat there for five minutes or so with an air of pleased attention, I would turn on them and curse them roundly for not pointing out that I was making mistakes. I have sometimes thought it would be an interesting experiment to conduct a retreat in the same way; to put in heresies all over the place and see how long it was before the retreatants started protesting. I'm not going to do that in this retreat; any heresies you may find me guilty of will have got there by accident.

However, what is more likely to need tapping than your faith is, I hardly need say, your character—your moral character. And when I say that, I don't want you to start thinking about the temptations which mostly distress you, which are most frequently mentioned in your confessions and most deeply regretted when you have given way to them. No, those temptations which occur in your weekly confessions, whatever danger they may have for you, have at least this relieving feature; you know about them and are on your guard against them; you don't slip into them unconsciously. What I'm thinking about now are the bad habits into which you do slip unconsciously, and which don't, therefore, figure in your confessions as much as they ought to.

I mean, for example, selfishness. Oh but, you say, I'm not selfish; it's quite a mistake to think that. Yes, of course you don't think you're selfish; nobody ever does. But how long is it since you last wrote home? . . . Well, there you are, you see.

I mean, for example, pride; in its commonest form, self-conceit. I know you don't think you suffer from that; but tell me, what do other people think about it? Have you ever wondered?

I mean, for example, laziness. And by that I don't mean just laziness about your school-work; you will hear all about that when you get home and the reports come in. I mean a whole habit of letting other people do things for you instead of doing them for yourself; a refusal to take any interest in things of the mind.

Those are the habits that grow upon us without our noticing them, as our life rolls on in its unthinking way; and that's where you need the retreat father's hammer to go tap, tap, just to make sure; only to make sure.

And of course, simpler and still more obvious, there's the question of our spiritual and devotional attitude. Our prayers, our confessions, our Communions; their frequency, the time we give to them, the trouble we take over them— is it quite all right? Does the wheel ring absolutely true? No harm in giving a tap, just in case. Well, you know, when I say that I am the man with the hammer, that isn't really a proper statement of the case. I should have to be a very clever person indeed if I were proposing to give just the right tap to every single one of you. Only, you see, it's a matter of common experience that it doesn't really matter very much what the retreat father says, as long as the retreatant listens, and waits for the odd phrase here and there which was meant for him. Divine Providence will see to it that the right tap comes, if you will listen for it; probably when I'm not meaning it at all.

I once wrote, on this subject, some words which strike me on re-reading them as profoundly true: "Each of us has, I suppose, his own wave-length in the supernatural order, and catches, if only he will listen, what the others miss." I once wrote a sentence in a detective story which had nothing whatever to do with religion, but it made a lapsed Catholic in Western Australia write to me and say that he wanted to come back to his religious duties. So I say, if any one of you gets any good out of this retreat, it will not be because I tapped; it will be because Almighty God tapped, using the hammer of your own conscience to do so.

Well, there's one very simple way of preparing our minds to take a retreat in the right spirit; and that is, to cast our minds back to the last school retreat we made, and institute comparisons between now and then.

Do you remember the name of the preacher who gave the retreat last year? Do you remember any single thing he said? Well, it doesn't matter. What I want you to do is to picture yourself as you used to be a year ago—that curious little boy you remember. The trousers you're wearing, perhaps, were made for *him;* how short they're getting! A year ago, you were still in So-and-so's class; your hands, perhaps, less washed, your hair less brushed than it is now; how you used to put food away then! What a kid you were! And now, take that kid and contrast him with yourself, with your present highly sensible, highly responsible, highly educated, immaculate self.

What difference is there, apart from outward details, between you and the grubby little thing you were a year ago? Did he feel bored, fed up with life, as often as you do? No? I wonder why. He wrote letters home, oftener than you, or less often? Was he, perhaps, less embarrassed, less awkward than you are when he saw his people in the holidays? What sort of reports did he get, as compared with yours? His conversation—was he more particular than you about the kind of things he said, the kind of things he talked about? His idle thoughts—were they less clouded by shadows than yours? His prayers, were they more, or less, regularly said? His Communions, his confessions, how do they compare with yours? His prayers, were they more, or less, regularly said in the twelve months between? Throw your mind back; remember where you used to sleep then, and what thoughts they were that occupied your mind; your place in refectory, and what you talked about; your place in class (where your name is perhaps still carved on your desk), what your work was like, and whether you cheated over it; your place in chapel, how much you talked, laughed, let your mind wander. . . . Reconstruct all that for yourself, and then come back to your present self, the perfect, the finished product, and make the comparison. What has happened in between?

It won't be the same story in every case. Some of you, as you look back, will be able to thank God unaffectedly for graces received, for bad habits got under. With others, it will be different. In this last year, bad habits have grown into sins, poses and tricks have become part of your character; you have become flabby and pleasure-loving, or perhaps hard and cynical, desperately anxious to be thought smart. You are older than you were then, and a little wiser than you were then; but are you happier? Is your life better planned, better controlled?

Would you change places with that kid of last year? No, of course you wouldn't; nobody at your age ever wishes that he was younger; that's only for old and tired people like me. But suppose he had died, by an unprepared death, just after last year's retreat, would he, do you think, have gone to heaven? Would his purgatory have been short or long? And now, if you were to die an unprepared death? How do your hopes of heaven, your chances of purgatory, compare with his?

I'm not suggesting that you should use this standard of self-measurement if you don't want to. Some of you will soon be leaving school; some of you have experienced an alteration in your lives during the past year, a severe illness or a family bereavement, and will like to approach the subject in your own way. But I do want all of you to look at your lives calmly, dispassionately, as if from the outside, during this retreat; without sentimentalism, without hysteria. Ask

yourself whether your life rings true under the tapping of
conscience; whether it has achieved the perfect circle you
want it to be, or has been pushed out of shape somehow—
by unrepented sin, by some silly pose or affectation, by care-
lessness, by refusing to face some difficult issue, some un-
resolved problem—and so has worked itself into a pattern
that is not really you. If you find that, then lose no time in
asking God to take your life and break it and remould it
according to his own plan; for you will find no peace, believe
me, and no satisfaction until you have learned to want to be
what he wants you to be—that and nothing else.

2 You've Got a Soul

YOU'VE got a soul. That means you're different from the
dumb animals. I know that sounds an ordinary thing to say,
but it isn't really quite as simple as it sounds. How do we
know, in our ordinary experience, what a soul is like, or
indeed that there is such a thing?

It's quite easy to see that you differ from a mineral, say
a lump of coal—or is that a vegetable? Well, say a lump of
lead. You differ from it because you grow and it doesn't.
You grow, whether you want it or not; your hair, for example, has to be cut at intervals (sometimes longer, sometimes shorter—the intervals, I mean) whether you want it
or not. It's easy to see you're something more than a mineral.
And it's easy to see that you're something more than a vegetable, though I daresay, when you are being particularly
stupid in class, your teacher throws doubt upon the point.
You differ from a vegetable because you can move about
from one place to another and because you can feel things.
A scarlet runner can't really run; you can. If somebody treads
on your corn, or hits you in the eye, you feel it; but if you
tread on a barleycorn it doesn't feel it; and if you hit a potato
in the eye, it doesn't feel it. But when you come to ask
exactly how we are different from the beasts, and how we
are better, it isn't all such plain sailing.

You see, so far as the powers of our bodies are concerned,

we share them with the beasts, and it is the beasts, not we, who excel in them. An elephant is stronger than a man, and a greyhound runs faster, and a cat balances better, and so on. Even at our own sports I imagine they could beat us if they had the practice—you wouldn't take on a monkey, for example, at throwing the coconut. I suppose we do see better than the animals; further than most of them and more accurately (for our size) than any of them; if you shew a kitten its reflection in a looking-glass, the odds are that it takes no notice—it isn't accustomed, as we are, to judge things by eye. And of course there's a whole world of art and beauty which belongs to us, of which the animals betray no consciousness at all. But then, if you told a dog that you were a better man than it was because you could see better, the dog might reply that there was no reason for you to think yourself such a dog because you saw better; hang it all, you can't smell nearly as well.

Perhaps some of you know Mr. Chesterton's poem in *The Flying Inn:*

> They haven't got no noses
>   The fallen sons of Eve,
> Even the smell of roses
> Is not what they supposes,
> But more than mind discloses,
>   And more than men believe.
> . . . .
> The brilliant smell of water,
>   The brave smell of a stone,
> The smell of dew and thunder
> And old bones buried under,
> Are things in which they blunder
>   And err, if left alone.
> . . . .

They haven't got no noses,
And goodness only knowses
The Noselessness of Man.

No, we can't state the difference between ourselves and the lower animals by making it simply a matter of sensitiveness.

The difference comes in because man has a soul; and if you go through the three powers of the soul as they come in the Catechism, you will find that animals either haven't got them, or have got them in a different sense from ourselves. The memory, for example. Of course it's obvious that animals have memory of a sort. But it will be a very crude sort. I don't know if you know the story of the North-countryman who was found one morning lying in a ditch, in an attitude which suggested that he must have been drinking rather freely overnight: the humorist who discovered him said, "Hullo! you look as if you'd been to a wedding yesterday." And his answer was, "Well, I don't rightly know whether it was a wedding or a funeral, but whichever 'twas it was a very great success."

That's what we call the animal memory—no particular recollection of place, date, or circumstance, but a comfortable (or uncomfortable) feeling inside which gives the impression that a recent experience has (or hasn't) been a very great success. Well, I suppose if a cat which had had a good square meal two hours before were endowed with a voice, like Balaam's donkey, it wouldn't be able to tell you whether it was a saucer of milk or an old hambone that it had been getting at, still less whether it had come by them officially or just pinched them out of the larder; it could only tell you that the thing had been a very great success.

But *you* have a memory, a human memory. The impressions that are left in it are not a mere disorderly series of

states of mind, but a continuous history with a plot and a
hero. What the plot is we shall see later, the hero is yourself.
Recall again that grubby little creature, so silly, so awkward,
so undeveloped, that you were this time a year ago. Yes,
that was you. Your body has been changing all the time:
the hair you then found it so difficult to keep tidy has all disappeared now and gone into sofa cushions or something;
that's a new lot you've got now. You've got a fresh set of
nails, and some of you have even had to shave since then.
And that's not all; the whole fabric of your body has been
changing, so that the scar you got when you cut your knee
has disappeared now, and a fresh lot of skin has come in
place of it: there's very little in your bodies that lasts out a
year or two. And yet you are the very same person. Your
faculty of memory unites for you the whole history of your
life, so that the fact of having cut your knee is a part of you
just as much as anything you did the day before yesterday—
the scar is gone, but the memory is a part of you.

And then, your intellect. One hears a lot from time to time
about the calculating horse and the learned pig and all the
rest of it (there are performing fleas, if it comes to that) and
old ladies tell you stories about the intelligence of their horrible little chows: "Wasn't it too clever of him? You know,
I really think Bimbo is the best friend I have. Just look at
his wistful little eyes; don't they look as if he was trying to
say something?" Very likely they do; in fact it's almost certain that he wants to say, "What's wrong with another
biscuit?" But you're too polite to say that. How I hate those
stories! One day I am going to write a vast work on the
idiotic stupidity of animals, and dogs in particular.

I'll tell you one thing I noticed that seems to me to illustrate very well the fact that animals have not got intellect
and we have. I stayed once in some country lodgings where

there was a dog that was for ever barking at me as if I were a burglar whenever I put my nose outside the house. Having discovered that the dog was firmly chained in its kennel, I used to shew a manly indifference to these protests. Then one day my host, its master, took me out to see it, and "Now," thought I, "the intelligent brute will see me chatting fearlessly with its master, and will learn to respect me." Not a bit of it; all the time we approached that fool dog went on barking its heart out. Then we went up, and its master undid the chain, and "Now," thought I, "this dog will be worth avoiding." Would you believe it, no sooner was the chain slipped than the silly brute came up and licked my hand.

You see what was going on in its ill-ordered consciousness? As long as it was on a chain, I was an enemy; the moment it was loose, I became a friend. In fact, it had wholly failed to grasp the distinction of subject and object in cognition. For when we think—even when the most helpless dud, who is always being asked by his teachers whether he has got any brain-pan at all, sets himself to think he can just distinguish between himself, who is thinking, and the thing which he is thinking about. The dog couldn't; it just had a feeling of "Enemy!" when its collar was on the chain, and a quite different feeling when it wasn't. Sometimes a very exceptional animal puts up a very good imitation of thinking, but animals don't really think: if they did, mankind would never have got ahead of the brute creation, and you and I would probably be engaged in keeping flies off the rhinoceros, or running errands for the giraffe.

Man, then, has a soul which expresses itself in memory and in intellect; it expresses itself also in will. There again, we have an affectation of talking about animals as if they had wills, but it's all nonsense. Sentimental ladies will talk about the cruel fox hunting down the inoffensive little rabbit, but of course really it would have been just as sensible to talk about the cruel rabbit hunting down the inoffensive little turnip. Animals can't be good and bad as we can. The greyhound that chases the hare isn't full of calculating malignity. No, the greyhound has only one thought, "Hullo, here's sport!" We're really talking nonsense when we say "Good dog" or "Bad dog". It's true that you can bribe a dog to do what you want it to do: that if you give it enough biscuits it will learn to risk death for the flag of your country. But when you've done that you haven't really made it a patriotic citizen; it's no nearer to thinking rationally than that caterpillar you found in the salad, is it? And you may succeed in discouraging a dog from chasing the hens by giving it the walloping of its life, but you can't really suppose that you've trained it into a humanitarian. You can't really reward an animal for doing right, or punish it for doing wrong; you can only bribe it to do what you want or choke it off doing what you don't want.

But in the case of human beings we do actually punish, we do actually reward, and in doing so we assume that human beings make a choice between right and wrong. A single, very homely instance will be enough to shew my point. Suppose three boys in my form fail hopelessly in the attempt to construe a passage of Livy. There you have a situation of almost painful realism. I tell each of them to write out the English of the lesson. With what motive? They themselves, of course, will tell you that it's because I've always had a down on them, but that's neither here nor there. The first, say, really did try to learn the stuff, and simply couldn't make head or tail of it. The second forgot (quite genuinely forgot, this time) that any lesson had been set. Now, so far, I am not in the proper sense inflicting punishment. I am making the first boy write out the English in the distant hope that he may remember something about it when it comes to the examination. I am giving the second boy a lesson which will remind him not to forget in future. But the third boy has really been slacking; has, through moral weakness, failed to learn what he could have perfectly well managed to learn: and him I do punish. The first boy I have to bludgeon as a donkey, the second I have to drive about as a goose; the third I punish as a man.

This soul, then, which betrays itself in memory, intellect, and will—what is it? Well, we can all answer glibly enough, "Oh, it's a kind of spirit". But remember, when you're saying that, you're not making your terms very much clearer, because if you come to think of it it's the only kind of spirit of which you or I have any sort of experience. Of course there's rum and whiskey and those things. But there you're using the same word in a quite different sense. Our souls are spirits in the same sense in which the holy angels, and the devils, and Almighty God are spirits. And of these other spirits we know only by hearsay. That's nothing for us to be surprised about, because we are still in the body. We may like it or dislike it, but here we are in the body, and it's only by means of the body that we can express ourselves or hold intercourse with one another. Now, what do we mean when we say that the soul is *in* the body?

Well, we don't mean that it's rolling about inside your chest, so that if you shook a friend hard enough you could hear his soul rattling. We don't mean that the body is a kind of bath-sponge, with the soul sucked up into it, so that it is squeezed out with a sort of squelchy noise at the moment of death. The meeting of soul and body is something absolutely unique in our experience, and probably unique in the whole economy of the universe. For it is the mysterious union of a material with a non-material substance. Soul and body are

made for one another; we haven't got here by accident. The
soul can exist without the body, and after death it has to, but
for all that they're made for one another. Theologians will
tell you that the soul is a kind of spirit which has an aptitudinality—that's a jolly word, aptitudinality—for a body,
but bless you, they don't know what that means. It's simply
a brute fact, and we've got to make the best of it.

You see, it is a frightfully important fact. If you were an
angel, you wouldn't have to lug yourself out of bed in the
morning to praise God; you wouldn't have to spend two or
three hours out of the twenty-four stuffing food through a
hole in your face; but, unfortunately, you have a body as
well as a soul. If you were a monkey, you could spend happy
afternoons throwing bananas at your grandmother, and
when you'd nothing else to do you could sit down and have
a good scratch at the back of your head; but, unfortunately,
you have a soul as well as a body. How we've been trapped!
What a joke it would be, if it weren't so serious! The angels,
of course, are too well-behaved to laugh, and the animals
are too stupid to see the point, but what a joke this half-
angel, half-animal would be, if there were anybody to laugh
at it!

We've got to make the best, as I say, of this curious position of ours. And there's this to be said, it's a very sporting
position. In war, when there has to be a liaison, a juncture
that is, between the armies of two different nations, it isn't
the worst but the best troops that are put in the gap between.
The holy angels praise God naturally, so to speak; they have
wills which are now confirmed in goodness. The dumb beasts
praise God naturally, because they've got no wills and they
have to praise him in all they do since everything he has
made is good. And we, too, are forced to praise him. But to
us he has given the choice, a real choice, whether we will
praise him like the beasts because we have to, or praise him

like the holy angels with the sacrifice of our wills. You see that, don't you, that Almighty God has done us extraordinary honour in choosing us to serve him in this strange, amphibious, soul-and-body existence of ours? Keep your powder dry: he wouldn't have put us here if he hadn't wanted us.

Let's take another side of the question—there are really quite a lot of sides to the question when you sit down to consider a quite simple proposition like "I've got a soul": the subject seems to branch out in all directions. Your soul is given you so that you can make something out of it. Of course, your body is too, but if you come to think of it you can't do much with your body in the way of altering God's handiwork. You can do setting-up exercises and short-arm balance and become a bit less flabby and a bit stronger than you'd be otherwise, but it's not much when all's said and done. Not much, I mean, if you compare yourself with a salmon, which may grow to fifteen pounds or may grow to forty pounds according to what it eats. And your face and appearance generally; you can oil your hair and get it to sit down at the back, at least some of us can, but when all's said and done you've got to go through life very much as God made you. Nobody ever consulted me as to what kind of nose I would like to have: it just grew that way.

But your soul is of a very different order. It's given to you to make what you will of it; to make it as white as snow or as black as pitch; think of that. If an old man in the street sold you an old bulb and told you that if you neglected to water it it would come up groundsel, but if you watered it twice a day it would come up a cherry tree, that would be nothing like as exciting, nothing like as romantic, as the excitement and romance of having a soul all your own to play with—God help us, how many of us do just play with it! And that's what God has given us.

Now, mark you, man is made in the image of his Creator,

and therefore it is his chief joy to create. That's why children
like building things. It's not that they do it the least bit well.
Have you ever helped a child to play with Meccano? Well,
don't; they're perfect fools at it. But they like to *feel* they're
creating. Even when they tear up the eiderdown it isn't because they want to destroy it; it's because they want to have
a ball of jolly woolly stuff to fool about with. That's why
grown-up people will absent-mindedly pile up salt-cellars
or match-boxes while they're talking; they must build. And
that's why artists are commonly selfish people; it's because
their job allows them to spend the whole of their time doing
what they enjoy doing, that is creating, instead of being a
bank-clerk, who isn't at liberty to create except in the even-
ings, in a garden sixteen feet by ten.

Now, in shaping the destinies of his own soul man is in an
extraordinary position; he is both the artist and the material.
Ordinarily, in artistic creation, you are hampered by the
stuff you have to deal with; the lines won't come right, the
colours will go all blodgy; the rhyme to that thoroughly
excellent first line won't come. But in deciding—under the
Providence and the grace of God—the destinies of your soul;
in writing that great drama, building that great edifice,
sketching in that picture, which is the history of an immortal
human soul, the material you are dealing with is you. You
are moulding, you are fashioning, a living thing, which is
yourself. That ought to be fun, oughtn't it?

And, remember, this work of art you are producing, your
own destiny, will take its final form at the end of your life.
There will be no time afterwards to put in finishing touches,
and introduce little alterations. As death finds your soul, in
the state of grace or out of the state of grace, so it must remain for all eternity. The needs of your body may seem very
pressing to you, but after all what are they? The body is, in

any case, doomed to corruption. Why, long before it actually dissolves, it grows feeble, and bent, and wrinkled, as if to announce its own transience. And yet, look at the way we worry about our bodies! Go into a chemist's shop and look round you at all the toothbrushes and the scents and the corn-cures and the throat-sprays and the baby-soothers and the fat-reducers and the nail-files and all the rest of it—wouldn't it make you suppose that this body of ours was going to last on to eternity, and it was the soul that was due to peter out in fifty years' time? And yet we know it's the other way about.

See how the Saints disagreed with our estimate! Some of them, I'm afraid, carried it rather far, and didn't see why they should worry about the toothbrushes and the nail-files, or even the cakes of soap. But *all* of them thought that our careless way of looking at the relations between body and soul was a silly one. Look at St. Francis; no one could be more human than he was or have more sense of fun, and yet he would go out and roll in the snow, and beat himself with the utmost good-will. He called his body "Brother Ass", and when he was going to take the discipline he used to lecture his body and say, "Now, Brother Ass, you're going to have a bad time of it"—rather with the air of a schoolmaster saying, "This hurts me more than it does you." And on his death-bed, you know, he apologized to Brother Ass for having flogged him so often, but pointed out that the thing really had to be done. Well, what are we to make of all that?

I'm not, you'll be glad to hear, suggesting that you should imitate the practices of the Saints all at once. The doctor would probably have something to say about your rolling in the snow, and as for flagellation, I daresay all you need for the present will be managed by other hands than your own. But this I do say, that for the last year you've been pampering and cosseting that body of yours, stoking it up and oiling it and running it about and getting it into condition and washing and brushing and overhauling and generally repairing it, and all the time your soul has come in for a good deal less of your attention. So it's your soul we are going to think about; and first of all, we shall be considering the End for which your soul was made, that is to say, Almighty God.

3 *Finding Yourself*

In almost any other kind of prayer it is your object, if you can and as far as you can, to lose yourself in God. In a retreat it is just the other way; what you want to do is to find yourself, and to find God by finding yourself. I daresay that sounds to you as if I was just talking any kind of nonsense, just saying the sort of thing it is my business to say without thinking what it means. Well, let us get it a little clearer. What do I mean first of all when I say that in a retreat you ought to want to find yourself?

If you meet Protestant friends in the holidays, and tell them that during the last part of Holy Week you went into retreat, they will perhaps ask, What exactly do you mean by that, going into retreat? Had you been doing something wrong, and did the priests shut you up in a dark room by yourself and feed you on bread and water? Or were you unpopular with the other boys, and did they send you to Coventry or something like that? And the answer is, No, once a year at school we retire from the world, because it is good for us. Now, we are not in a position to retire from the world in the good old thorough-going way which was fashionable in the early centuries. In those days, their idea of retiring from the world was to go off into a desert somewhere for five or six years, and live in a draughty cave on dates or anything that came handy, and spend your time weaving baskets. I think you would have enjoyed that even less than you enjoyed your last retreat (or are enjoying this). But that was the idea of it, to get away from the world and isolate yourself from it, so that you could find out what your self was really like. After all, that is what you do in any chemical experiment; you try to isolate some substance so that you may get an idea of what its true nature is in isolation from its usual surroundings.

And that is what we are meant to do in retreat, only in a school retreat we generally do it rather imperfectly. There is a rule of silence, of course, which some of us keep well, others not so well; but we do not really get away from each other's company. As you sit there, I doubt if you feel isolated from the world. The boy on one side of you has a cold, and is breathing heavily through his nose with an unpleasant snorting sound; the boy on the other side of you is sharpening a pencil and the chips keep falling into the turnup of your trousers; and you have a first-class view of the collar of the boy in front of you, which invites your attention because it has come loose from its stud. All that distracts you, and makes you more than ever conscious of your neighbours, just when you ought to be concentrating your attention on yourself. However, you have got to put up with that; there is not enough room in the grounds of most schools to let each of you go off into a separate corner by himself and weave mats, without the temptation to tickle somebody else with the straw. You have got to make the best of it, and try, in the middle of all these distractions, to find your selves.

Well, one way of finding yourself is to go and look in the looking-glass; that will answer various important questions such as, Is my tie straight? Have I got a smut on my nose? But that is not the kind of reflection which I am recommending to you at the present moment. That external appearance of yourself is a thing you are all sufficiently familiar with; even the plainest of us has to face up to the looking-glass fairly often. And your body is a thing which you probably give quite enough attention to as it is. If you were to reckon up all the time you devote in the course of a single week to pampering your body in one way and another, washing it and brushing it and combing it and greasing it and filling it up with food and drink and exercising it and then allowing it to sleep off the exercise you have given it, you would be surprised at the total of the trouble it had cost you, this body which has only got to last you a matter of eighty years or so at the longest, whereas the soul has got to last you all through an eternity. And how much attention does your soul come in for during the same space of time? How often do you bring that up, so to speak, before the looking-glass of conscience, and consider what *that* looks like, or whether conceivably there is anything wrong with *that?*

Anyhow, it is your soul that has got to come up before the looking-glass this time. And, you know, that is not such an easy thing to manage. For this reason, that your outer self, your body, is only one self, whereas your inner self, your soul, is no less than three. At least, you may perhaps say that your body is two selves; there is the front view, which is what you see in the looking-glass, and there is your profile, which your friends see, but you mostly don't. How terrible it is, isn't it, to catch sight suddenly of one's profile? At least, if you have a profile at all like mine. But if, as I say, there is one view of your exterior self with which you are unfamiliar, the side view; in this business of your soul, your inner self, there are three different points of view, only one of which you are accustomed to contemplating at all. There is your self as you see it. There is your self as your neighbours see it. And there is your self as God sees it.

Your self as you see it. You know that person, don't you?
All too well you know him. That figure so little appreciated,
so much misunderstood; all his teachers seem to have a down
on him, it is difficult to see why—they imagine, for example,
that he does not do as much work as he might; they imagine
that he is inattentive in class, when the fact is that he is just
a little tired, that is all. And the boys are not much better;
they seem to have got hold of the idea that he is conceited;
that he is greedy about his food—greedy, I ask you!—and
that he loses his temper easily, which of course is a perfectly
ridiculous thing to say.

And meanwhile, this interesting figure, yourself as you
see him, has so much that makes him an absorbing subject
of study, if people would only go the right way about it. Not
too many brains, perhaps; he gets a bit lost when making a
speech at the debating society, for example, but on the other
hand, what a man of the world he is! Not much that you can
tell him which he doesn't know, when it comes to the practical side of life. What a good sense of humour he has! Not
that he enjoys the silly jokes some people make, but he can
appreciate real wit. And one great thing about him is that
he has no silly sentimentalisms or affectations; he sees things
just as they are, and looks out on the world in a plain, business-like way. If he has a fault, it is that he is too good-
natured, too unselfish, too unwilling to take offense. But
there, I must not go on detailing to you all the excellences
that are to be found in your self as you see it; it would take
me too long; and besides, you have only to think for a while
in order to supply the full list for yourself.

And then there is your self as other people see it—curiously, that is not quite the same thing. Has it ever happened
to you that, by overhearing some chance remark you were
not meant to hear, or through some friend repeating to you

a criticism which he was not meant to repeat, you suddenly got a glimpse of what the world says about you behind your back? It is a strange and sometimes a humiliating experience. I do not mean you would hear, in all probability, anything very damaging to your character. But if you could overhear one of your school friends being interrogated about you during the holidays, his criticism would probably be something like this: "Oh, he's all right; bit of an ass, you know. We pull his leg a good deal. Extraordinary chap; never seems to know when you're joking." No, not a very damaging criticism, but somehow strangely unlike the estimate we heard just now. And yet it is the same character, seen from two different points of view. But there is a third point of view all the time—your self as God sees it.

And that is the point of view you want to realize, the point of view you want to enter into, when you go into retreat. Concentrate on that; don't worry about other people; put blinkers over your faculty of attention, and enter into yourself. You are probably expecting me to say that God sees your soul as a crawling mass of corruption, almost unrecognizable under the disfiguring effect of your sins. I am not going to tell you that; I have no means of judging that. It is perfectly true that God knows your faults, and knows the heinousness of your faults, far better than you can yourself. But it is also true that he knows the excuses for them better than you do yourself; knows your weakness when you are too proud to admit yourself weak, knows your temptations when you are too blind to realize that they were temptations. No, we will talk about sin later on; for the present I want you to see how God's point of view about you differs from your own, differs from that of your neighbours, simply because he is God, because he made you and knows you and has a use for you and a destiny for you to fulfil.

God sees you at once as something infinitely small, and something infinitely important. Infinitely small—he might have created you without creating the world, but he didn't. Infinitely important—he might have created the world without creating you; but he didn't.

Did it ever occur to you to wonder, when you were quite small, whether you were not the only thing that really existed; whether all the people around you, your nurse and your aunts and the gardener's boy and the man who came to wind up the clocks, were not really just so many shadows, put there to fill in the picture and amuse you? Whether all the trees that showed against the window-panes, and the garden wall, and the pond with the tadpoles in it, and all that sort of thing were not just a sort of background which your eyes saw, but which had no existence except in your eyes? I know that it sounds a very silly speculation, but I assure you that there have been, and are, people calling themselves philosophers who really believe that. And it is a very handy thing when you are arguing with such folk, to be able to say, "Yes, that idea did occur to me, but I gave it up at the age of five."

Now, suppose that were true; suppose there were only one creature that existed—you; and all the rest of the universe, the sun and the moon and the stars and every created object outside yourself of which you have ever had experience, were just something in your imagination. It would be like that passage in *Alice Through the Looking-Glass* where the Red Queen says it would be very uncomfortable for Alice if the Red King woke up, because Alice herself is only part of the Red King's dream. If the whole world were just a dream, and you were the dreamer of it, and it had no existence in God's sight except as a part of you, you would still be, in God's eyes, something infinitely small.

You see, he made you out of nothing; he can remember you when you did not exist. You know what a sense of inferiority it gives you when old friends of the family come to stay, and embarrass you by telling you that they can remember you when you were so high, and that they frequently saw you in your bath. It seems to put them at an unfair advantage, that they were already grown up and full of worldly wisdom when you yourself were quite young and had to take your bath in public. What sense of inferiority ought we to have, then, when we compare ourselves with God? He existed, when we were nothing, when we were only an idea, so to speak, in his mind; and he brought us out of non-existence into existence—could anything put us at a worse disadvantage than that? Something infinitely small, his creature; even if he had created nothing besides or if he had created nothing besides except for our instruction and amusement.

But as a matter of fact the multitudinous bulk and variety of the universe around us warns us to remember how small we are. All these suns, and systems of suns, in existence, and we only the inhabitants of one tiny planet. All those innumerable people who have passed through the world centuries and centuries ago, all the millions of people who are living in the world now, black men and white men and yellow men, bad men and good men, sane men and lunatics, and of all those people, nearly two thousand million of them, you are just one—that does not make you feel very important, does it? And yet, unconsciously, you always behave as if you were the only person out of all those millions that mattered; you grumble about the cold that spoils *your* holiday, or the warmth that spoils *your* skating, the rain that interferes with *your* picnic or the sunshine that interferes with *your* fishing. That then is one difference between your self as you see it and your self as God sees it—he sees you as something infinitely small.

And at the same time—that is the curious thing—he sees your soul as something infinitely important. As I say, it would have been a perfectly possible thing that you should never have existed. If you were ever shewn the place where your father first met your mother, did it occur to you to reflect that but for that meeting you would not be in existence? And, if I may be pardoned for dispensing with empty compliments, the world would have got on quite well without you? If you had never been born, the boy or girl on your right in school would be sitting now next to the boy or girl on your left, with more room in between them—that is what it comes to. Everything would be going on in the world just the same; the spring would be starting and the buds shooting and the holidays coming on; and I should be sitting here saying exactly what I am saying now, only there would be no *you* to listen to me. That whole world of seeing, hearing, touching, suffering, sinning, loving, hating, which has you for its centre and its subject, would never have been; but the world outside you would have suffered no loss—or let us be charitable and say next to no loss.

But as a matter of fact you do exist—God has called you into existence; he wanted you, meant you to exist. Only one more soul among all those millions of souls, yes, but he wanted just that one; he shaped a life for you, an environment, an education, circumstances, natural gifts, an eternal destiny. You were the subject of his loving forethought, no less really, no less deliberately, than if you had been the only thing he had created. Your body, indeed, is part of the general sum of matter in his universe, shaped by natural processes; but your soul is a special creation; he repeated, in creating your soul, that act which first brought the sun and the stars and the heavens into existence. And it stands to reason that if God took all that trouble over you, so to speak —it is a meaningless phrase really, but you see the idea— if God created you so deliberately, thought of you as an individual person, he thinks of you as an individual person still. The Almighty Power, whose word sways the whole of creation, does make you the subject of his loving regard, just as if there were no other human creature in existence; will do so always, unless you die an impenitent death. You remember how the shepherd in our Lord's parable, when he had lost one out of a hundred sheep, went into the wilderness and sought diligently till he found it? So it is with you; God cares about you as if he had nobody else to care for.

God is to be thought of as a Person in this very practical sense, that he knows us, loves us, and does things for us. And the reason why we are persons, why God made us persons instead of stones or trees or animals, is the same—that we may love him, serve him, and do things for him. That is what we are for; that is our characteristic birthright as human beings.

To know God; that does not sound, at first, an easy thing to do. When we say that we know a human friend, or that we have come to know him better than we did, what do we mean? We mean that we have been talking to him, or that we have been writing letters to him at least, and that his words, or the expression on his face, or the less trustworthy impressions we can derive from a letter written in pen and ink, have served as an index of his character. Now, we do not get to know God in that way. We cannot see him who is of his very nature invisible to mortal eyes; no accents from him fall upon our outward ears. Nor does he even give us signs of his presence and of his activity, no signs, I mean, beyond those which he has given to the human race in general through this creation which is the work of his hands. And yet we want to know God, not merely to know that he exists. We shall not be satisfied with a mathematical demonstration; we shall want to get to know him, to appreciate his qualities and to feel at home in his presence.

How are we to do that? Well, I will not speak yet of the revelation which he has made of himself in the Incarnation of his Son, nor of that special intimacy with himself which he grants to us in the holy Eucharist; we shall come to that later on. For the present, I will only say this; that you will get to know God in proportion as you do your best, whether in your times of prayer or out of your times of prayer, to put yourself in his presence. To recollect yourself, I mean, before you begin to say your prayers or when you settle down in your place in church, or even at odd times of the day when you have nothing to do for the moment and are thrown back upon yourself; to recollect yourself—to reflect that God, who is Spirit, is directly present to your soul, which is also a spirit, and that his influence manifests itself in every motion of your will, in every thought which races through your brain, and to do your best to realize that and let it dwell in your memory.

To love God, that is an easier idea to entertain, but not an easy thing to do, if we would make our love of him in any way worthy of him. After all, when you love a human friend, it means so much in your life. It means that you appreciate his qualities, and want other people to appreciate them as you do; that you cannot bear to stand by and hear him criticized or belittled; that you take delight in his presence, and not only in his presence, but even in things which remind you of him; you trust him, so that you would have no secrets from him, would let no discontented thoughts come between you and him; you feel yourself unworthy of his friendship, you defer to his pleasure; you do not like to be long away from him, and when you are away from him, your mind is full of the thought of him, and the mere thought brightens your work and soothes your disquiet. And if we were like the saints, that is what we should feel about God. Probably we shall never attain anywhere near to such intimacy as that; but that is the aim we must set before ourselves in loving him, and until we achieve it we must confess to him, always, that we do not love him enough.

To do things for God, to serve him—that will follow naturally from our love. It is possible to serve God by reminding ourselves that he is our Creator, and we ought to do his will as unquestioningly as dumb brutes obey their masters. Or we can serve him by reminding ourselves that he is our king, and that any homage which we offer to him is only his right. Or we can serve him by reminding ourselves that he is our captain, and that it is the first duty of a soldier to obey orders without asking to be given reasons. But the best way of all is to serve him because he is our friend, because we want to protest our love for him by our actions, and are sorry, sometimes, that he gives us so little chance of proving ourselves worthy of his friendship.

That is what God made us for, his human creatures, to be his friends, his personal friends. Not that he has need of our friendship; for his infinite beatitude would have remained unaltered if no soul had ever been breathed into a human body. But his overflowing Love is constantly forming new reservoirs, as it were, which it can fill with a human love that makes a response, however poor a response, to itself. As the single orb of the sun is reflected anew, whole and complete, by every puddle on the road-side, so in each insignificant human life the all-embracing love of God shines down, as if it had no other scope or aim for its self-fulfilment, and desires as far as our human imperfections will allow it to find its own image reflected there.

4 *Personal Religion*

I WANT to make sure of leaving something, however little, of a definite impression on your minds, before this retreat comes to an end. That is not quite such an easy thing to do as you might suppose.

I happen to know that, because I once gave a retreat in a school where I had given one five years before. Some of those who heard it were still there; I could name one at least. And I fancy that if I had asked him there and then to stand up and tell us how much of that five-year-old retreat he still remembered, his reminiscences would not have detained us very long. I have talked about it at Oxford to boys who heard it, and always with the same negative results. One says, "Yes, I can't in the least remember what you said, but I know *I* rather enjoyed it", just putting a little too much emphasis on the word "I", so as to make quite clear that if he did enjoy it, he was the only person present who did. Another says, "Oh, yes, I remember that retreat of yours perfectly; there was something about—let's see, what was it, now? Oh yes, I know, there was something about an Arabian palace." One of them was quite confident that he must have been ill or away at the time; he had no recollection of my ever giving a retreat, and he was certain that if he had been there he would have remembered the circumstance. . . . So he told me; but the other day he was looking through an old diary he kept at school, and found he had been there after all.

No, I don't imagine that any of you will remember much about this retreat, five years from now; time, the great healer, will have obliterated it from your minds together with the other unhappy memories of youth. But I would like to leave something behind, if it were only a single phrase, if it were only a couple of words.

While this retreat lasts, I want you to have a kind of motto, a kind of label, continually before your mind's eye as the lesson of every conference I give you and the key-word of every consideration I suggest to you. And that label, that motto, is to consist of two words, PERSONAL RELIGION. If people ask you what this retreat was about, you will be able to tell them, just in a couple of words, "Oh, he was talking about personal religion."

I daresay that those two words do not explain themselves very well. Some of you are probably wondering how a thing like religion could be described as personal, some of you are unable to understand how religion could be anything but personal. Let me explain a little; I mean by personal religion a religion that affects you personally instead of affecting you externally. And if you press me further, and want to know what is the difference between being affected personally and being affected externally, I think I can make that clear by an illustration.

A great public figure, let us suppose the King if you are English or the President if you are American, is dead. He is not a relation of yours; you have never met him, you have never experienced any act of kindness from him. You knew him by his pictures, by his reputation, and that was all. Your real reaction to the news may be, "What, is he dead? Poor old chap." And yet somehow it seems the right thing to do to make a fuss about it and get excited about it. Now, all that isn't exactly hypocrisy. But it is an attitude which we have to adopt deliberately, it isn't an emotion that comes natural to us. We are sorry, but we feel sorrow only because good taste and good feeling seem to dictate it—it is not really ours.

Now, contrast that state of mind with the state of mind which some of you have been in before now—not many of you, I hope—the state of mind you are in when there is bad news from home; when somebody you are really interested in, somebody you really love, lies sick, and there seems to be small chance of recovery. You will not make any parade of your anxiety, while you are with your friends; it would be bad form to pull long faces and to go about the place moping, when the anxiety that gnaws at your heart affects you only, and not those around you. But all the time, the news you have just received has, for you, blotted out the sunlight. Your food has no taste for you, your pleasures have no attraction for you, work is more than ever a tedious burden, company is a nuisance, conversation an effort to you, because all the time there is a picture at the back of your mind —a picture of somebody you love, far away, battling between life and death. You are not trying to force yourself into an attitude, to school your emotions; rather, all the effort you employ is to keep your emotions from running away with you. It is as if part of yourself were suffering, instead of someone else.

That is what I mean by the difference between a thing which only affects you externally and a thing which affects you personally. Now, what I want you to consider in this retreat, as far as God gives you the grace to read into your own heart, is just this, What is the quality of my religion? Is it something personal to me, or something external to me? Something external to me, like the loyalty which I feel, or feel that I ought to feel, towards the King or the President? Or something personal to me, like the love which I feel for those whom I love best on earth?

I call it external religion, if a person regulates his spiritual life in accordance with his surroundings, and alters his habits of devotion the moment his surroundings alter. You say your prayers when you go to bed in a dormitory, where there are other people about to see whether you say your prayers or not; what happens when you get home, and sleep in a bedroom by yourself? You go to Communion so often in term time, when there is a habit of going to Communion among those around you; how often do you go during the holidays, when those conditions are relaxed? I call it external religion, when you think of religious observances merely as a performance to be gone through, not as anything which you value or would be sorry to do without. If you were wrecked on a desert island, and found that it was impossible for you ever to hear Mass, how much would you mind? Would you be sorry as Sunday after Sunday went by, and never the sound of a Sanctus bell; or would it give you a sense of relief, like not being able to wash your teeth because you had lost your toothbrush? I call it external religion, when a person only remembers to say his prayers if he is in a hole,—if there is an important game on, or if he has got into a row, or if he has to enter for an examination, and knows that he has not done enough work to get through.

You see, all that means that you let outside circumstances control your religious actions, instead of being free, instead of controlling your religious actions for yourself. Whereas, if you had a personal religion, it would wear the same in all conditions, in all company, in all weathers; or, if circumstances made it impossible for you to follow your ordinary habits of devotion, you would be sorry about it, you would feel that something was missing in your life—that is what I mean by a personal religion.

If I were talking to Protestants, I would not bother to say all this, because it is roughly true nowadays to say that Protestants have either a personal religion or none. When you leave school, and go out into the world in which most of the people you meet are not Catholics, you will be surprised, I think, to find how much religion there is, and how little religion there is, among your fellow-countrymen. And the reason is simple—those non-Catholics who have any religion at all have a personal religion; they value it; it means something to them. Whereas those non-Catholics who lose their personal religion lose their religion altogether. They don't even pretend to go to church; they don't even go through the form of saying their prayers. As soon as they leave school, they cease to behave as Christian people. Many of them are very good people; many of them live self-sacrificing lives and set before themselves high ideals. But unless they have a personal religion already, religion ordinarily means nothing to them, once they have left school.

With Catholics, it's different. Unlike Protestants, they have behind them centuries of history; their religion is a tradition nineteen centuries old, and they are not going to drop it easily. Unlike Protestants, they are fortified by the consciousness that there are millions of other people in the world believing what they believe, worshipping as they worship; they are not so easily influenced by the fashions of the world around them. Unlike Protestants, they have a religion which is divine in its origin, and offers unique opportunities of grace. And a Catholic who has really no personal religion, or next to none, may continue all his life to be a practising Catholic, may receive the last Sacraments on his death-bed, may find his way, so we hope, to heaven, all owing to a religion which is really external to him, which has never bitten deep into his life or made itself part of his most intimate thoughts.

Of course, you may say to me, "I don't see much wrong with this external religion you talk about; it looks good enough for me. I am a Catholic, and I hope to live and die a Catholic, but you mustn't expect me to get excited about my religion, because I'm not that kind of person; I'm quite satisfied to remain in class B, to run my religion on second gear all my life." If you take up that sort of attitude, I've no more to say to you. At least, I have a good deal more to say to you, and it will take me about four hours to say it, but I don't suppose it will interest you much. I will only make three comments on your point of view. First, that that kind of religion is not the kind of religion Jesus Christ meant Christianity to be. Next, that that kind of religion is not worthy of a human being. And, thirdly, that it is not a safe kind of religion to practise nowadays, and in the country we live in; it is very easy to lose that kind of religion, and to lose your immortal soul while you are about it.

First, I say that it is not Christianity as Jesus Christ meant it to be. I remember a boy at the school I used to teach at who was asked, in an examination paper, to give the context of the verse, "Do no more than that which is appointed to you." In case you have forgotten it, perhaps I ought to explain that when the soldiers came to St. John the Baptist, and asked him how they ought to amend their ways, he said to them, "Do no more than that which is appointed to you." But this boy gave as his answer, "This is what our Lord told his disciples when they asked him how they should inherit eternal life." It would be hard, if you come to think of it, to get an answer more exactly wrong. What our Lord said was, "He that loveth his life shall lose it." What our Lord said was, "What shall it profit a man if he gain the whole world and suffer the loss of his own soul?" What our Lord said was, "He that doth not forsake father and mother and take up his cross and follow me is not worthy of me." That was his religion—something which came first, something which mattered supremely, something which did make you get excited about it, sometimes even turned your whole life upside down. Nobody is going to realize that ideal, unless his religion is something personal, not something merely external to himself.

Next, I say that this external religion is not worthy of a human being. It is man's privilege to live by his ideals. He can live without ideals, but his life is the poorer for it; he will never know the joy of living if he lives like that. It is natural for a man to have some kind of work in life, some kind of job which is his job; if that job is mere drudgery to him, if he does it only because he has to do it, without getting interested in it or losing himself in it in any way—well, he will make a livelihood, but he won't really live. It is natural for a man to marry; it is quite possible to marry a woman you aren't the least bit in love with, to live quite contentedly and to bring up a family without having ever known what it is to be in love—I say that is possible, but it is not natural, it is not what marriage was meant for. And if it is a warped life, a stunted life, which finds no zest in God's gift of work and no joy in God's gift of marriage, what shall we say of the life that finds no joy and no zest in the greatest of all God's gifts, the opportunity he gives us, here on earth, to know and to love and to worship himself?

In the third place I say that, even if you are a Catholic, to be satisfied with an external kind of religion is to run a risk, and a grave risk, of losing your religion altogether. If your religion isn't rooted deep—our Lord himself has warned us about it in the Parable of the Sower—the chances are three to one against the seed of faith ever bearing any fruit in your life. A religion that is external to yourself may do all right as long as everything goes well with you, but it won't stand a shock. You will come up against difficulties about the faith, and you will not be sufficiently interested to take those difficulties to a priest or to think them out for yourself—you will let your religion go. You will come up against some temptation which will sweep you off your feet, or the prospect of some worldly advantage will encourage you to be false to your religion, and it will go. It will go, because it is not part of you, because it is something at the circumference of your life instead of being the centre of your life. That is the danger.

A school can teach you your religion, but it depends upon you what is going to become of it afterwards. While you are at school, the routine of your life makes religion easy for you; custom makes religion easy for you; human respect makes religion easy for you; but all that will be no use unless you make some effort, on your own part, to realize the meaning of the religion you are being taught here and to make it your own. That is why, in this retreat, I want you to take stock of your religion and to see where you stand. "Is my religion personal to me, or is it merely external to me?" That is the question I want you to ask yourself, and to entreat Almighty God to shew you where the true answer lies.

5 *The Reality of God*

I HOPE I am right in assuming that most of you, although in
other ways you may not be given to scholarly tastes, have at
one time or another read a detective story, possibly more
than one. And it is a curious thing about detective stories, if
you come to think about it; they are not worked out like
other stories of adventure; in fact they are worked out as
nearly as possible the other way round. I mean this, that in
the ordinary stories of adventure the incidents develop naturally one out of another, and usually come thicker and
thicker as the book goes on; so that all the time, as you finish
one chapter and go on to the following chapter, you are
wondering to yourself, "What will happen next?" Who is
going to get hit over the head with a sandbag next? Who is
going to be thrown out of an aeroplane next? You are looking forward all the time to something that *is going to happen*.

But in a detective story it is the other way round. The
crime happens, and if it is a really good detective story that
means that the murder happens, in chapter two or thereabouts; certainly not later than chapter three. By the end of
chapter three, if not earlier, the central incident of the book
has already taken place. There is your dead man lying in
the beautifully upholstered study of a country house, his
face all bashed in so that the features are unrecognizable,
apparently by the use of some blunt instrument; the door is

locked, the chairs are thrown about all over the place, there is a half-empty bottle of cyanide of potassium lying on the floor; people have been coming in and out at the window without taking the trouble to wipe their boots; there are two cigar-ends and a whole quantity of cigarette-ends lying about; there are thumb marks on the inkstand and on the mantelpiece, bullet-holes in the wainscoting, a pool of blood close to the door—in fact, one way and another, it is clear that something sensational has been happening on the night of Tuesday; we know that *something* has happened, but we don't know *what,* and the interest of the book really lies in finding out what did happen, something that had already happened by the end of chapter three.

In the same way, if it is a good detective story, all the more important characters have already been introduced into the story in the first chapter. In the ordinary adventure story the characters come in gradually one by one as the story proceeds; in the detective story they all crowd on in the first chapter or two, so that we may be thoroughly in the dark as to which of them has committed the murder. There is the dead man's wife, and his daughter, and the young fellow she is engaged to, and all the other guests who are staying in the house, and the private secretary, and the governess, and all the servants, from the aged butler who has been with the family for sixteen years down to the chauffeur who happens to have gone away that night to see his widowed mother. And the excitement about all these people to us is not, in the detective story, "What are they going to do?", but "What *have* they been doing?" Which of them was it that handled the blunt instrument with such fatal precision? Which of them was it that left the diamond tiara lying under the roll-top desk?

And now I want to suggest to you some ideas about the oldest detective story in the world. And the oldest detective story in the world is the world itself.

Of course, it is perfectly possible to regard this world in which we live as an adventure story. Even in the few thousand years during which his records have come down to us, the history of man, with his triumphs over nature, his inventions and his discoveries, is one of breathless excitement, and it is impossible for us as we look forward to the next chapter, still hidden from us in the mists of the future, not to be wondering "What will happen next?" And especially in times like these, when things move so rapidly. After all, I am not so frightfully, frightfully old; but I can remember well enough the days when wireless telegraphy simply was not thought of and the idea of flying with machines heavier than air was regarded as a foolish daydream. It is quite easy to understand, in days like these particularly, how there are people who look upon the world simply as an adventure story, and are fascinated by the attempt to anticipate what *will* happen, what developments will take place in the next chapter of history.

But all the time, remember—and that is what we are concerned with this morning—the world is always and must be a detective story as well. There still remains the riddle, unsolved for us apart from religion, "What *has* happened?" How did we get here, who put us here, and what are the terms of our tenancy? Here is the world, this great ball of matter, lying about like the corpse in a detective story, all unexplained; a great ball of matter, slightly flattened at the ends as if by the use of some blunt instrument; and all about us those sparks of light which we know to be other worlds, but which look to our eyes like smudges in the sky, finger-prints, you would imagine, left by the Author that we might be able to trace his work. This world, scarred all over with the effects of those great upheavals, from glaciers and volcanoes and all the rest of it, which took place, so it seems, hundreds of thousands of years ago. This world, so complex and so untidy in some ways, and yet bearing such unmistakable marks of purpose in the laws which organize it. All through human history, men's minds have been dazzled and baffled by that problem, which they may despair of solving, but can never wholly give up.

And in this great detective story, man himself is the detective. He wants to know, not merely out of inquisitiveness, but because he must find the answer to the riddle if he is to know what is his place in the created universe and what, accordingly, are the duties of his state. Before he answers the question, What am I to do here? he must answer the question, Who put me here? But there, of course, you may object that I am going too fast. I am assuming that the world could not have existed unless Somebody had put it there; that it could not have existed unless Somebody had created it. How do I know that, you ask? May it not simply have been lying about there from all eternity, of its own accord, so to speak, without any first Cause, without any Creator? That is what the materialist asks, and he proposes to explain the existence of the world by attributing it to blind chance—that is what it comes to; by saying that it was not created at all, it just happened.

That, of course, is a silly explanation; it is like the easy explanation in the detective stories, the wrong explanation which looks obvious and is only meant to catch the mugs. It would be an unsatisfactory explanation, even if this world, this created universe of which we are speaking, were no more than a lump of matter. But if you come to think of it this universe does not merely consist of a lump of matter; it includes mind as well, the mind of Man, which is immaterial, which has its own inner life independent of the sensations which it derives from the body. Now, as far as the scientists can tell us anything, when the material universe started there were no human minds in existence. And to suppose that the immaterial mind is just a sort of by-product of matter would be mere childishness.

For the mind belongs to an entirely different and higher order of existence. Your mind—well, I daresay hard things have been said about it before now, especially by the people whose business it is to import education to it. But your mind is a bigger thing altogether, a more important thing altogether, than Mount Everest or the British Channel. Neither the British Channel nor Mount Everest could have any importance at all unless there were minds for them to have importance for. So that the existence of matter does not explain the existence of mind; it must, somehow, be the existence of mind which explains the existence of matter. And that means that Mind must have been in existence before matter ever came into existence. Whose Mind? Not yours or mine; we were not born or thought of all those hundreds of thousands of years ago. There must have been, in the very beginning of things, a Mind from which the whole material universe took its origin; and it is the creative Mind that we call GOD.

That is the only solution of the great detective story which satisfies the very conditions of the problem. There must have been a creative Mind at work. And remember, when all is said and done a Mind means a Person. You will find that many modern writers, desperately anxious not to commit themselves beyond what they are quite certain of, will talk about God in the neuter instead of the masculine; will ascribe the creation of the world to Something instead of ascribing it to Somebody. They will tell you of that great Source from which all being takes its origin; of that Cause which lies behind the operation of all natural causes; of that Force which inspires all life in the world, of that all-embracing Spirit which pervades and organizes the whole of existence. Now, it is perfectly correct to speak of God as a Source, or a Cause, or a Force, or a Spirit; but what these people are for ever trying to do, unless you watch them carefully, is to forget that God is a Person and treat him as if he were only a thing. And that is nonsense.

I say that is nonsense, because it is false to all our experience. We have and we can have no conception in our minds of origin, of causation, of force, or of spirit, which is not derived from our experience of persons. The source of a river is not really that from which the river takes its origin; it is only the hole in the ground from which it comes up. The cause of any event is itself due to a series of causes behind it; a force is only that which imparts to something else motion which has already been imparted to itself. The only experience we have of originating things, of causing things, of exercising force, is the experience of our own nature in its manifold activities. And similarly the word Spirit means nothing at all unless it means a personal spirit, for all the spirits we have ever known were personal spirits, you and I and so-and-so and all the people we have met—we have come across spirits only because, only where, we have come across persons.

That, then, is our starting point; the riddle of existence, the great detective problem of existence, demands as its only possible answer the existence of a personal God. The world as we know it could not have come into being if there had not been a personal God there to account for it. Now, what idea are we to form in our minds of a personal God? There are some notions connected in our minds with personality which will have to be ruled out. For example, we have no experience of a spirit which has no body attached to it; you and I, unless we are in the habit of seeing ghosts, do not profess to have seen a disembodied spirit. But we cannot think of the Mind which created the material world as attached to a material Body; for if so, who created that Body? We are subject to the influence of passions; we get angry or depressed or excited; we cannot imagine God as subject to passions like that. He is without body, without passions; he is present everywhere; in all those ways and and in many others he is unlike persons as we know them. And yet he is a personal God; what does that mean? Why, you can put it quite simply, like this.

Supposing you were on a desert island, one of the comfortable desert islands that you read about in stories; with plenty of telescopes and gunpowder and all that; turtle and other nice things to eat, a watertight cave to live in, clothes as good as the climate demanded, and a dog and a parrot to play with—what would be your complaint about the desert island? Well, I suppose some of us would find it hard to get on without the pictures, and the illustrated papers, and so on; but your chief grievance, surely, would be that there was nobody else there. Nobody to know, and nobody to know you; nobody to love, and nobody to love you; nobody to do anything for, nobody to do anything for you. To know one another, to love one another, to do things for one another—those are, if you come to think of it, the three bonds which unite us as human beings together as persons. And all those marks of personality exist in God; he knows us, and we can know him; he loves us, and we can love him, he does things for us, and we can do things for him.

And the first step towards having a personal religion is to believe in God as a personal God and behave towards him as a personal God. It is really extraordinary how many Catholics there are who don't seem to realize that, or at any rate do not behave as if they realized that. They know all about it, of course, in theory; they can answer the questions about it in the Catechism without making a single mistake. But to know about a thing is not necessarily to realize it; that is the whole trouble.

It is quite true that all Christian people believe in a God who is personal. But I do not think it is quite true to say that all Christian people realize the fact, or treat him as a personal God. Let me explain what I mean—you say your prayers, sometimes, with great fervour, when you have got into a row, or when you have done something wrong and hope that you will not get found out; or when there is a game on or an examination—generally speaking, when you have something to gain by it. It is quite right that you should; but you see, don't you, that so far a personal God is being no use to you. Suppose—it is an impossible supposition, but just suppose—that there was a magical talisman in your possession (like Aladdin's lamp), which would give you exactly what you wanted if you whispered some magical formula into it. That would be just as good, for your purposes, as saying your prayers—indeed for your immediate purposes it would be better, because it would be sure to work every time, whereas you cannot always get what you want by praying for it. And if you only pray to God when you want to get something out of him, it looks rather as if you would just as soon have that magical talisman instead.

Again, you find yourself from time to time tempted to commit an action which you know to be very sinful. And you say to yourself: "No, it would not be worth risking hell for that." Quite right that you should; but you see, don't you, that so far you are not treating God as a personal God. If there were, on the other side of the grave, some vast machine which automatically consigned all the good people to heaven and all the bad people to hell, like the escalators at an underground station, that would be quite sufficient reason for you

to be afraid of going to hell when you died, without Almighty
God coming into the question at all.

And once more, it is possible even to worship God, or at
least to go through the outward forms of worshipping him,
and even so not to treat him as a personal God. I mean, you
go to Mass on a Sunday morning; but what exactly do you
mean by that? How much is there of a conscious response in
you to the mysteries which are taking place? . . . After all, it
is the thing to do, to go to Mass on Sunday; your ancestors
always used to do it, your friends do it; the neighbours expect it of you; people have been doing it all these hundreds
of years, so presumably there must be something in it; and
after all it is good for a man to humble himself sometimes
before the unseen things that lie beyond the grave; it puts
him in his place; it gives tone to his character. People who
never go to church are apt to become rather bumptious and
self-opinionated people. Yes, that is all true; but if that is
all your reason for going to Mass, you have not really de-
clared your belief in a personal God. You have genuflected
before the altar, yes, as a soldier salutes the colours; but did
you really mean anything more by it? If God were merely an
abstract idea, like the greatness of your country or the ideal
of human progress, would you have shewn him any less respect than that? Yes, it is possible to worship God, and still
not think of him, in your heart of hearts, as a personal God.

That is what I am so afraid of—that if you do not learn
to get on terms of closer intimacy with him while you are at
school, or if, when you have left, you leave behind you the
enthusiasms of your school days, and feel ashamed of the
trustful love with which you approached him in your school
days, you may grow up into a Catholic who has no personal
religion. One knows so many people who seem like that—
God forbid I should say that they *are* all like that; it is such

a mistake to judge by appearances—but there are so many people who *seem* like that; who pray, but only for what they want, and because they want it, not because they want to come close to God; who live decent lives, but more for fear of some expected terrors after death than with any idea whose laws it is that sin disobeys, whose majesty it is that sin outrages; who go to Mass, but only by force of custom, unintelligently derived from the traditions of their family, or from the conventions of those among whom they live. Is it for that that we send boys to Catholic schools, and lavish such treasures of care upon their religious education?

God is not a mere mascot or talisman, to help us get the things we want. God is not a machine which automatically distributes punishments and rewards in a future life. God is not an abstract idea, summing up under a convenient formula the highest aspirations of the human race. God is a person, who knows us, who does something for us.

He knows us, he knows all about us—naturally, because he is everywhere. When we are told that God is everywhere, that he sees us at every moment of our lives, it is apt to give us a rather dreary, uncomfortable sort of feeling. We picture him as a great Policeman, or an officious Schoolmaster, who is always hiding round the corner waiting to pounce out upon us, so to speak, when we have done something wrong. What an idea to have of God! He is not somewhere hidden away out of sight; he is there all the time; he is in this room just as really, just as literally, as you or I. Consequently, he knows all about us; he understands us absolutely. That means, it is true, that he knows a great deal to our discredit, which the world at large is not allowed to know. But it also means that he understands our temptations, our weaknesses, more thoroughly than we even know them ourselves; can make allowances for us, as not even the closest of our friends would dare to do. What a comfort it is to have a friend who knows us in and out, with whom it is not necessary to keep up any shams or appearances, who will never misjudge us, never mistake our motives! Such a friend we have close to us at all times, if we would only believe it; it is God.

He loves us—yes, that is extraordinary, knowing all about us as he does. Yes, that is extraordinary, seeing that he has no need of us, and that nothing we can ever do or say could ever materially add to the glory and the blessedness which he enjoys in heaven. And yet, have we really any right to talk like that? Can we really pretend that the people we ourselves are fond of are the people for whose character we have an enormous admiration, or the people from whom we have received great kindnesses? Is it not the common experience that the people we are really fond of attract us we cannot tell why, some chance resemblance, some hardly realized point of contact with ourselves? God loves you, because he sees all the time his own image in you; will see it there always, however much it may be covered up and disfigured by your sins, unless you remain finally impenitent and are eternally lost. How rare are those friendships which no neglect on our side can destroy! Yet such a friendship each one of us has in this life; it is God's.

He does something for us; rather, he does everything for us. But for his merciful design in creating us, none of us would ever have seen the sun's light or breathed the air of day. And, having created us, he holds us in being from moment to moment; there is no breath that we breathe, no play of our muscles, no thought, even, that flashes through our minds, that could ever come into being without his co-operation. And he is not satisfied with that, with these gifts that bring happiness to us here. He wants to have us always near him, and he invites us to share his own happiness in heaven;

for no worthiness of our own, for no virtues of our own, but simply from the fulness of that abounding love which must find an outlet for its benevolence even in us creatures, even in us sinners. A Friend who knows us, who loves us, who is determined to make us happy—that is God.

6 *The Presence of God*

WE ARE all apt to feel a bit out of our depth when theology
crops up, and quite right that we should. But at the same
time, I think it's important to start our retreat by a little
straight thinking about Almighty God. No, it's all right, I'm
not going to make it difficult. But I want to suggest that there
is a right and a wrong *attitude* towards Almighty God, and
it's our instinct, if we are not careful, to fall into the wrong
one.

You see, when we are small, and even when we have
grown up and gone to school, the people who talk to us about
God are mostly parents, nurses, governesses, schoolmasters,
and people in authority over us, who are a bit apt to rein-
force their authority by an appeal to theological sanctions.
There's a story about a small girl in an American railway
sleeping-car. The sleeping-cars are long corridors like res-
taurant cars, with curtains over the berths, so that when you
undress you have to do it in bed; an uncomfortable performance, as I dare say some of you know. In this carriage, everybody had finished undressing, and the lights were put out.
And the small girl, who wasn't accustomed to the dark,
started calling out at intervals, "Daddy, are you there?
Mummy, are you there?" And this had been going on for
some time, when an angry gentleman in the top berth of all
leaned over and said, "Yes, Daddy's there, Mummy's there,

and I'm here, and we're all trying to get to sleep; so for heaven's sake stop that confounded noise!" After that there was a short interval of silence, and then the small girl's voice was heard again saying, "Mummy, was that God?"

An angry Voice out of the dark, from somewhere up above, telling us not to—that is the notion of God we get, some of us, from the circumstances of our early training; and no wonder if we shove away this unwelcome thought into the back of our minds. It is folded away there, pigeon-holed, and only brought out for certain special occasions, when we realize that we can't get on without it. The ordinary Christian wants to conjure up the thought of God on three separate kinds of occasion; when he wants to get something by prayer (we have already said something of that); when he is depressed; and when he has the misfortune to fall into sin.

Surely that's a very extraordinary thing, when you come to think what God is and what we are; that we should only want him to exist, now and again, for our convenience, instead of trying to realize that he is there all the time? That *is* what we are doing, you see, all of us; we are *afraid of God*, which is not at all what the Bible means by "fearing God". If we are to become better Christians, we have got to conquer that phobia, that shyness, as far as possible—we shall not get rid of it altogether. Shall I tell you what it reminds me of, this God-shy attitude of ours? It seems to me we are for all the world like some strange pet, a mongoose or something like that, which is only half-tamed. Come and meet it with a saucer in your hand, and it is all over you; the rest of the time, it runs away.

Don't think, then, that I am merely offensive if I invite you to compare yourself with the dumb animals. That is sometimes a dangerous line to take in a retreat. I expect you all know the story of the pious book which included a meditation on the subject of Palm Sunday. "Point one," it began, and talked a little about the ass on which our Lord rode, and the colt which followed her. And then, "Point two—The colt follows the ass; do you always follow your spiritual director?" Don't let's talk about donkeys this morning; let's talk about dogs; after all, the human race has succeeded in taming the dog better than any other animal. I always like Bishop Challoner's note about the dog which followed Tobias on his travels, and ran ahead to announce his return home, wagging its tail. He says, "Things that appear minute [in Holy Scripture] have indeed a deep and mysterious meaning about them." I wonder what deep and mysterious meaning dear Bishop Challoner found in the little Toby-dog.

But if I were asked to find a mystical meaning about the word "dog", I should point immediately to one obvious fact —it is the word "God" spelt the other way round. As if to shew us that there is a kind of proportion sum involved; as God is to man, so man is to dog; or, if you prefer it, as dog is to man, so man is to God. Our position in respect of God, who means so much to us, whose ways we understand so little, is very much the same as the position of a dog in respect of its master. Let's apply that to what we said about the rare occasions which force us to conjure up the thought of God in our lives.

The first occasion I mentioned, you will remember, is when one wants something rather badly, and turns to God in prayer about it. What ought our attitude to be? Well, let's think of a dog as you see it when dinner's on the table; when I say a dog I mean a real dog, not a Pomeranian or a Pekinese. What very different ways they have of begging for food, and how much nicer some of them are than others! A dog with really bad manners will come up and yap at you, but of course that's awfully bad form. The most that a reasonably well-bred dog is allowed to do is to sit by your chair and turn its head to watch every mouthful you eat, as if to hint that there are other people hungry besides yourself, and sometimes to give a little yawn as if to make sure you realize that its mouth does open.

A slightly better technique than that is to sit very quiet indeed beside the person you regard as the most likely source of nourishment, and every now and then (you need to be a large dog to do this) put your paw on his knee as if to say, "You haven't forgotten I'm here, have you?" But the best kind of dog doesn't even do that; it just sits with its chin against your leg looking up steadily in an admiring sort of way, giving the impression that of course you are much the nicest person in the room and obviously you know best, and if you should have a bit of that gristly part to spare so much the better; if not, of course, it doesn't matter. I met a dog some time ago that was a perfect specimen of this kind of approach; it didn't get anything because I never feed other people's dogs, but it was far too polite to shew the least sign of disappointment.

Well, I don't want to press the parable too far; but we are most of us, don't you think, rather like the ill-mannered kind of dog when there is something we want badly and we are praying to get it? We get all strung up and hysterical about it, and we fidget and squirm and our breath comes short and we almost bark out our Hail Mary's as if God wasn't attending to us and we could make him attend to us by shouting at him; and one way and another we try to throw ourselves into our prayer, as if we could force him to do what we wanted. We almost behave as if we thought that it was all an effort of will-power on our part, something like cranking up a car. Well, is there really any reason to think that sort of thing does any good?

Long ago, I was either at the Zoo or at some circus, I forget which, and there was an elephant there which would take a penny from you with the end of its trunk and put it into the automatic machine which dropped scent, as far as I remember, on your handkerchief. Well, I suppose I must quite innocently have given it a bent coin, or a halfpenny, by mistake; anyhow, the machine didn't work. And the elephant cocked its head on one side, and then lifted up its trunk and gave the automatic machine an enormous whang in the stomach. And when even that didn't do any good, it put its trunk into the slot where the pennies went in and blew down it. Nobody ever believes that story, but I know that it's true because it happened to me. Well, you may say if you like that it was a very sagacious elephant to think of all that, but it was a limited kind of sagacity; it thought that force would do the trick, when obviously force wouldn't. What was needed was just the right kind of penny with the right amount of weight. And it's the same with the kind of prayers I've been talking to you about; there's nothing wrong in approaching God like that, but I don't think it's the best kind of attitude in our prayer.

Surely two things are quite certain about making our requests to God. The first thing is—our Lord tells us about it again and again—that we must come to him in a spirit of confidence, feeling sure that he can grant our request and that he will if it is in the long run the best thing for us. And the second thing is, that prayer isn't merely a matter of bending God's will to ours; it is, much more importantly, a matter of bending our will to God's.

To adore and to desire God's holy will in everything, that is surely the real aim of prayer; if not, why did our Lord teach us to pray "Thy will be done" before we went on to ask for our daily bread or to have our trespasses forgiven?

So I think we ought really to model ourselves on what I called the best kind of dog; our attitude ought to be one of waiting, quite peacefully, quite humbly, with the intention we are praying for recurring, perhaps, at intervals to our minds, but in the main just letting the thought of God's sovereignty and his love sink into us and take possession of us. We ought to pray quietly and steadily, as the flame of the candle we have lit burns quietly and steadily before the image. I have the obstinate belief that God grants our prayers more readily, when he sees that they are not being prayed in a spirit of impatience.

Well, that's enough about that; we must go on to the next kind of occasion which drives us back upon the thought of God; and that was, if you remember, when the world seems to be treating us hardly and we feel down in the mouth about it. Now, I've nothing whatever to say against falling back on the thought of God at such times; obviously you couldn't do anything better. But what I do want to ask is this—Why should it need a touch of sadness in our lives to take us back to God? Why don't we equally, at times when things are going well with us and we are feeling really contented with life, take *that* feeling and lay it at God's feet, share it with God?

Let's go back to the dog, and remember what it's like to go for a walk with a dog which has a certain amount of companionableness and retrieving instinct. It doesn't stick close to you all the time and keep on nearly tripping you up, like the more boring kind of spaniel; no, it careers about all over the place, quite on its own, but it's always referring things to you, if you see what I mean. You are nearing a cross-roads, and it comes rushing back to you and then back again to the sign-post, trying to guess which road you are going to take. It comes across something really exciting, say an old boot, and it comes running up to you and says, "Look here, here's something really jolly; I'm sure you will be interested in this!" And if you kick a stone, even by accident, immediately *that* stone becomes something quite different from all the other stones in the road and much more important, and it must be brought back and put down in front of you in case you might want to kick it again. The dog is really taking its own walk, but it wouldn't dream of doing it without you; the whole fun of a walk, from its point of view, is to have a human being about to whom it can *refer* everything it comes across. All its adventures would lose their zest, but for you.

I hope it isn't difficult to apply that parable. Surely if we are really going to be Christians our life ought to be a walk with God; his near presence ought to be the inspiration of it, everything in it ought to be referred to him, not merely our bad times, when we rather ungenerously come to share troubles with him because we can't share them with anybody else, but our times of happiness as well. When you get a day off work, when you are going away for a holiday, when somebody gives you a present you've been wanting badly—the lightness of heart which you feel at such moments ought to carry your mind straight up to God. No need to pray, exactly; just let the thought of your own happiness mingle with the thought of God's goodness; learn, for once, to be grateful.

And again, we ought to refer to God our perplexities; when we have to make a decision of any importance, it ought to be second nature to ask the Holy Spirit to guide us right; and yet, how very few Catholics do that! Of course, at school, we don't have many decisions to make for ourselves; other people are apt to settle our lives for us; but you do get the chance of making some decisions, or you will before long. The undergraduates I had to look after at Oxford were always wanting advice about what career they were to adopt, most of them wanting to be part-time journalists, I gather, at a vast salary; but not one of them ever asked me to *pray* for the right guidance of his choice.

I don't mean that, when we have to decide on anything, we should simply pray about it and then toss up; we are not meant to dispense with human prudence, of course. There is a jesting story told about an Anglican bishop. He was offered a more important diocese; a lady called at the Palace and asked one of the daughters whether her father was going to accept the preferment or not; to which her reply was, "Oh, Father's in his study, praying for light, and Mother's upstairs packing the boxes." . . . I don't say we shall always choose unselfishly because we have prayed; but never to pray at all over our perplexities is surely less than Christian. Archbishop Butt used to tell the story of a small street-boy going to confession who accused himself in the words, "Bless me Father for I 'ave sinned; frown mud at trams and don't believe in the 'Oly Ghost." The temptation to throw mud at trams is one which many of us are spared; but really I don't think the rest of his confession would be unsuitable in the mouths of some ordinary Catholics.

Well, so far I've been trying to suggest that we ought to be more dog-like in the way we offer our petitions to God; and that we ought, dog-like, to refer to him, share with him, all the enjoyment we get out of life. If we do even that much, we shall be a little nearer to treating him as he deserves to be treated. But there was a third kind of situation, if you remember, which threw us back upon the thought of God; and that is when we fall into sin. The suggestion that I want to make about that is fairly obvious—it is a pity we should live so little in God's sight that we are apt to fall into sin *and then remember him.* How much better it would be if we lived so much in his sight that we remembered him all the time and therefore didn't fall into sin! Like keeping a watch and remembering to be in time for one's engagements, instead of hearing the clock strike and being reminded that one is late.

But is it possible to think about God all the time? Let me give you one last picture of dog-life. Think of a dog lying on the floor in its master's sitting-room, when he is taking no notice of it at all, but just writing letters, say, at the table. The dog isn't looking at him; it's half-asleep, and the images that race through its brain must be the images of its own dog-world. But if his master gets up for a moment to stretch his legs, or even reaches out to get his engagement-book down from a shelf in front of him, the dog pricks up its ears, looks up, and perhaps beats on the floor with its tail two or three times just to shew it's there still. It isn't actively attending to its master, because after all it doesn't understand anything about what he's doing or what pens and ink are for. But it has a kind of *habit* of attention to him, which becomes act on the least provocation. So it is with really holy people; they can't actively attend to God all the time; they have sums to add up and trains to look out for like the rest of us; but they have a *habit* of attention to God; he's never far from their thoughts, and the least little thing reminds them of him.

Yes, but is that any good to you and me, who aren't holy people? Well, let me tell you this; I think we could all cultivate the sense of God's presence a little more, if we sometimes deliberately allowed ourselves to think of him, made room for the thought of him. You are waiting a minute or two for the train—you read the advertisements, such advertisements! You are walking down, alone, to the football field; you must be humming a tune, or kicking stones all the time; why? Because, you say, I must have something to occupy my mind. I wonder whether we oughtn't rather, in those odds and ends of time which continually come our way, to leave our minds deliberately *un*occupied, so that the thought of God can crowd in? It will, you know, without any effort on our part, if we will just keep still. But we won't keep still; we search for distractions, instead of letting the thought of God come in and distract us. You try, sometimes, whether that doesn't work, and if it does try it a little oftener; make almost a habit of it. If you will allow yourself, even occasionally, to remember that God is there, you will be surprised to find how much easier it is to live as if he was there, there all the time.

7 *Our Lord's Life*

Do YOU often get depressed? The popular belief, of course, is that people of your age never *are* depressed, and have no reason to be; "alas, unconscious of their doom the little victims play," and all the rest of it. Why should you be depressed, in the spring-time of life, tasting it with the clean palate of youth, all the world in front of you, and no income-tax? Time enough to grow discontented when you turn into an elderly failure like me. Most of us when we get to middle age, feel rather failures; you've set out to do this and that, and your performance doesn't satisfy yourself, let alone other people. And other people are kind enough to write and point that out.

But when I try to look back at my own school days, I seem to remember great mountainous fits of melancholy which used to descend upon me; sometimes without visible cause, sometimes because I had set my heart on a thing and hadn't got it. I remember once failing to get a scholarship for which I was the obvious favourite, sitting down and reading the whole book of Job through, which I bet you've never done. I had a friend with me who was feeding me crystallized plums, because he thought they were the most likely thing to meet the case; and I ate them, of course, but without getting any complete balm for my injured feelings either from the crystallized plums or from the book of Job. Quite possibly I was a

morbid sort of youth, and it might have done me all the good
in the world if they had psychoanalysed me a little. But I
suspect that a good many of you know those moods of de-
pression, and it is with those in mind, particularly, that I
want to talk to you about our Blessed Lord's life on earth.

There was a school-boy I used to know, a Catholic, but
one who hadn't been very well instructed in religion, who
was responsible for a curious piece of theological comment.
He was travelling in very snowy weather, just before Christ-
mas; and when he'd spent some time looking out at the snow
drifting past the carriage windows and lying thick in the railway cuttings, he turned to the person who was with him and
said, "Hard lines on the Virgin Mary, wasn't it?" I don't
apologize for quoting that rather irreverent phrase, because
it illustrates so admirably, I think, the attitude which most
people who are not Catholics have to adopt towards the
whole story of the Gospels. The whole thing was, if you come
to think of it, awfully hard lines, awfully bad luck.

It was bad luck, to be sure, for our Lady and St. Joseph
that the Nativity should happen in winter, and when they
were on a journey, and when there was no room for them
in the inn at Bethlehem. But, if you come to think of it, it
all goes much deeper than that.

That Almighty God should not merely become Man to
save us from our sins, but that he should begin his earthly
life like the rest of us, as a little child with all the weaknesses
of childhood—that was bad luck. Full of human needs, and
expressing those needs at best only by signs; needing food,
and warmth, and protection! Surely, if there is such a thing
as bad luck, that was very bad luck indeed. And that wasn't
all; you'd have thought that when he came to earth he would
be born in a palace, with all the dignity of an earthly king,
all the respect and notoriety which such a position would

bestow; no state, no honours, no public attention could be too much, surely, for one who was Almighty God. But no, you see, it was bad luck there again. He came, indeed, of royal ancestry, but it was a very long way back; his parents were working-class people, and as we said just now they were living in uncomfortable circumstances at the actual time when he was born. And the place where it happened was just a little bit of a town in a remote province of the Roman Empire called Judaea; that was bad luck too, wasn't it, that he shouldn't have been born in Rome, the capital of the Empire, so that all the world would have taken notice and known about his coming. God not merely becoming Man, but becoming a little Child, born of very poor parents in a little forgotten provincial town—you could hardly have worse luck, could you, than that?

So much for our Lord's Infancy; and when you go on from that to the thirty years of his hidden life, things aren't much better. What waste of a life, we say, when somebody who might be doing really important work, really specialized work, is condemned for some reason to a drudge's task, which anybody else, so you feel, might have done equally well. A friend of mine was playing golf some time ago at a course near Oxford with Lord Nuffield, the man who makes the Morris cars. As he drove out from Oxford my friend noticed that there was something wrong with his car, something not very important; and over the luncheon table he said to his host: "Look here, as I've got to drive you back to Oxford after our game, I wonder if you'd mind ringing up the works at Cowley and having a man sent over to put my car right." So Lord Nuffield said, "That'll be all right," and when they went out afterwards in front of the club-house he said, "That your car? Well, just wait a minute", and he took off his coat and climbed under the car and mended it. My

friend asked if he would take sixpence for it, and he was de-
lighted; he said it was the first tip he had had for mending a
car since the days before the 1914 war, when he used to keep
a little bicycle-shop in Oxford. Well, that makes a rather
gracious story. But what should we think if the man who
was capable of designing all those engines and working up
all that gigantic motor industry had, for some private reason of his own, refused to do all that and insisted on spend-
ing all his time in a little shop in Oxford, mending punctures
in bicycle tires?

But what is all that in comparison with the career of our
Lord Jesus Christ? Here is Incarnate God come down to
earth, to bring back a sinful world to himself. And what does
he do? Why, for thirty years he spends all his time in a carpenter's shop; the Eternal Word of God making chair-legs.
All this vast amount of work to be done; all these sinners
to be converted, all these sick people to be cured, and our
Lord does nothing about it at all. Do you remember the man
at the pool of Siloe, who was paralysed, and had been waiting there thirty-eight years in the hope that he might be cured
one day? Well, for thirty out of those thirty-eight years our
Lord was going about on the earth, and every year he went
up to Jerusalem, but it was only when he was thirty years old
that the palsied man was introduced to his Deliverer.

Why did all that happen? We don't know; there may have
been ordinary human reasons which would partly account
for it. It may have been that St. Joseph couldn't get on without an assistant, and was too poor to get a hired assistant,
so that our Lord as a good Son found himself obliged to stick
to his work in the shop. Or it may have been—I've never seen
this suggested, but I don't know why it shouldn't be true—
that our Lord was saving money all the time he worked in
the shop, saving up money so that he would be able to pro-

vide for himself and his apostles (Judas among them) when he went about preaching and doing good. But whatever the reason, there is the fact; our Lord only had a short life on earth, and for rather more than ninety per cent of the time it looked as if he was making no effort to redeem the world at all. The world's Deliverer, set down to make chair-legs in a carpenter's shop; that was bad luck, wasn't it?

And if our Lord had bad luck—so we have decided to call it—in the circumstances of his birth and in the nature of the occupation which he took upon himself, he had bad luck too in the kind of people he met, the kind of people he had to live amongst. You see, he claimed to be the Son of God, claimed, that is, to be personally Divine. And the Jews above all people were slow to take in that idea, because they were so jealous for the honour of the one true God. To the heathen world, the doctrine of the Incarnation was not so difficult; when St. Paul and St. Barnabas performed a miracle at Lystra, the crowd immediately said, "The gods are come down to us in the likeness of men," and proceeded to do sacrifice—it seemed to them quite natural; but the Jews couldn't understand the idea in the least.

Our Lord had bad luck in the time when he made his appearance, a time of great political tension, when the Jews wanted a revolutionary leader who would shake off for them the yoke of the Roman Government; and our Lord didn't mean to do anything of that sort. He had bad luck in the part he came from—Galilee, which the Jews of Judaea looked on as a kind of half-heathen country. He had bad luck in the town where he was brought up; Nazareth seems to have been a sort of joke. So wherever our Lord went he was misunderstood. They said he was a provincial—"Can any good thing come out of Nazareth?" They said he was self-indulgent—"Behold a man gluttonous and a wine-bibber". They said he kept bad company—"This man receiveth sinners and eateth with them". They said he must be a madman—"He hath a devil". Even his own close relations didn't believe in him. Even his chosen disciples were always forgetting the lessons he had taught them, and having to be taught all over again. Did ever a man have such bad luck in the kind of people he had to deal with?

Well, I hope you all realize that so far we have been talking perfect nonsense. It is nonsense to talk about good luck and bad luck when you are discussing the earthly life of the Incarnate Son of God. Before the worlds were made, he chose for himself just those conditions; that humble birth, which is a rebuke to our pride; those years of drudgery and obscurity, which remind us of the value of the hidden life of prayer; that career of struggle and of misrepresentation from which we see that true success always comes out of failure. To make the sacrifice of his Life complete, he annihilated himself, so far as that was possible to Almighty God. What I want you to see is that your own life, the life which lies in front of you, is equally a matter of Providential arrangement; there is no good luck and no bad luck about it. You will suffer from defects of birth and early education; you will be given work to do which will be tedious and seem unworthy of you; you will meet with misrepresentation and misunderstanding on the part of your fellow-men. All that, in order that you too may make of your life a sacrifice, to be offered in union with his; that you too may learn to annihilate yourself, as far as that is possible to imperfect man.

Of course, we don't worry so much now as people used to in our Lord's time about whether a person is born in a palace or a stable. We have all become so democratic that we think all men are equal; or if they aren't they ought to be. At least, there ought to be equality of opportunity; nobody should start handicapped. That's all very well, but of course it isn't possible. You aren't all equal; you didn't start equal. Some of you stutter, some of you are short-sighted. I'm not saying that it's necessarily a disadvantage to stutter; it means, anyhow, that you don't very often get put on to translate in class. And as for being short-sighted, breaking your spectacles is generally good enough to get you off four days' work. No, all I am saying is that people do differ from the start; there are circumstances of birth or of very early education, circumstances over which we have no control, which determine very largely for us what our life is going to be. Some of us are good-looking; others will always find it a bit of a strain to face up to the looking-glass in the morning. Some of us are strong and healthy; others have to be careful about putting on an overcoat when they go out, and aren't hearty enough to get any fun out of playing games. Some of us are naturally sharp, and have a good head for work; others always hang about at the bottom of the class, even when they make heroic efforts to do some work. Life is a handicap race, even at school.

Of course, I think we're sometimes apt to make rather too heavy weather of the disabilities we suffer from. Most of us, really, are less stupid than we think; and—well, I won't say most of us, but a great many of us, do much less work than we think we do, and could really become far less ignorant if we really tried. And they tell me that it's the same with one's bodily strength, and that these physical exercises one does are calculated to develop the muscles in an extraordinary way. I used to do that kind of thing at my prep school, and I'm bound to say that my muscles always seemed quite as flabby at the end as they did at the beginning. Probably we didn't do the right kind; I don't think we used to waggle our middles about in quite the way you do today. Anyhow, if you stick to it, there's a chance you may get stronger. But my point is, anyhow, that when we've done all we can to become wiser and stronger and more beautiful, we still remain very much what we were to start with. The handicap is still with us; other fellows will get ahead of us, as a matter of course.

And when we come up against that sort of thing, we are inclined to say, Bad luck! It was bad luck So-and-so didn't get that prize; bad luck that So-and-so didn't marry the girl he wanted to marry, because the other fellow cut him out. Well, what I want you to see is that bad luck is the wrong word for it; and, worse than that, it's the wrong idea for it.

It isn't bad luck at all; it's God's design. He put you into the world to offer your whole life as a sacrifice to him in union with the perfect sacrifice of our Lord Jesus Christ. He knows the handicap you start with; of course he does, because it was he who put it there. He makes allowances; of course he does, because he meant those handicaps to be the condition of the sacrifice you were to offer to him. When he became man on earth, he might have been the son of an emperor, but he became the son of a carpenter; he might have been born in a palace, but he preferred to be born in a stable. It wasn't bad luck; he preferred it that way, because it made his sacrifice more perfect. And every disadvantage you started life with is, in the same way, part of his plan. It is to make your sacrifice to him more perfect; that is the meaning of it.

Well, those disadvantages of which I've been speaking are disadvantages you've begun to feel already; the physical disadvantages which come to you from the circumstances of your birth and your early childhood. But as for the second kind of disadvantage I was speaking of—being put down to do a dull job and a job you aren't fitted for—that will only come later on. What's that? You think it's a pretty dull job learning French verbs, and quadratic equations? Believe me, that's nothing to the dulness of the job you'll probably have to do later on, if you're lucky enough to get a job at all. Don't imagine for an instant that everybody older than yourself has found, and feels that he has found, his right niche in life. Every second person you meet is convinced that he could do some other job better, and grumbles about the job he has got. And you may find yourself stuck down in an insurance office with a fortnight's holiday in the year, although you are convinced that what you ought to be doing is writing sonnets or driving aeroplanes or something quite different. And when you mention it your friends will say, Bad luck. But it won't be bad luck; it will be just part of your sacrifice to God. Our Lord could have done anything he liked, or nothing if he'd liked; earth and sea and air obeyed him, and he spent all the best years of his life making chair-legs. Your job in life is not what you would do best or what you would like to do most; it's what God wants of you; your sacrifice to him.

And there's the third point. It goes without saying that no human being is ever thoroughly understood by other human beings who come in contact with him; and most human beings, if they are at all sensitive to what other people think about them, are conscious of being thoroughly *mis*understood. You know that already; you will be lucky if you don't, later in life, have a more searching experience of the same trial. You will meet with neglect, and misrepresentation, and suspicion; and you will perhaps know what it is to be let down by friends you have trusted. And all that will be bad luck, in the world's phrase. But once more, the world's phrase is the wrong phrase. It wasn't bad luck that our Lord lived despised by his enemies and died abandoned by his friends; he chose that. And whenever it falls to your lot to meet, at the hands of your fellow-creatures, with any passing shadow of that contempt which he experienced all through his life, it is not bad luck; it is because he has chosen that for you, in order that your sacrifice might be made more perfect—that is, more like his.

"As my Father hath sent me," our Lord says to his followers, "just so I send you." And our Lord was sent by his heavenly Father, how? To be born in a manger, to work in a village shop, to die on a cross.

8 *Sin*

SIN is the only thing, if you come to think of it, that man has invented for himself. Don't talk to me about aeroplanes and submarines; it was God who gave us aeroplanes and submarines; every bit as much as bread and coal. But sin is due entirely to man's own initiative—at least, the devil had a hand in it, but man got the credit of it. There's a story of a small girl who got in a bad temper and pulled her governess' hair and spat in her face and slapped her. And then of course there had to be an interview with her mamma; and her mamma, who liked to make the most of a situation of that kind, because she was pious, said, "You know, dear, who it was that taught you to do all that?" "No; who?" "I'm afraid, dear, it was the devil that taught you to do all that." And there was a slight pause, and then the small girl said, "Well, he may have suggested pulling her hair, but the spitting and the slapping were entirely my own idea." And I think you can say that if it was the devil who taught us to sin in the first instance, we've been a credit to his tutorship. It's a dreary subject.

Sin is the only thing in the world that really does harm. Of course, there are a lot of unpleasant things in the world which don't come directly from our sins; there are diseases and accidents of all sorts, and there is a great, great deal of harm done by well-meaning people. But that doesn't really matter. When we take up a newspaper, the world seems full of calamities and alarms; and we feel terribly worked up and anxious about what is going to come of it all, and what the state of the world will be in twenty years' time. But even if the human race were driven into a tiny corner of the globe, and all the rest of it were overrun by octopuses or white ants, it wouldn't matter as sin matters; for the earth will come to an end one day anyhow, and the whole of this visible creation will look like last year's model. But the consequences of sin will go on, go on, hurting people for ever. That's why I say sin is the only thing that matters.

How much more pleasant it would be if we could just go on talking about God, and how good he is, and how we ought to love him, and how we ought to try and think about his presence at all times. Instead, I've got to remind you about your sins. Not that I know what they are, but I've got to do my best. I am very fond of the story about the curate who thought he knew French. It was always rather a joke in the presbytery, and when one day a lady arrived demanding to have her confession heard in French they naturally fetched him down and said it was his job; it would be all child's play to him. So he sat down in the confessional, and all he heard on the other side of the grille was a voluble stream of French conversation of which he couldn't understand one word. But he was determined to make the best of it, so he drew himself up in his chair and said in a very severe voice, "Oh, vous avez, avez-vous?"

Well, that's rather my position; I can only talk to you about your sins in general; I don't know what it is that's worrying you. Even if I had you all sitting there in front of me, I still could not read your minds. If I were St. John Bosco, now—he used to run a kind of ragged school with about four hundred boys in it, and every night in his dreams he had a revelation which told him the exact state of the conscience of every boy in the building. So when a boy came to him to confession before Mass, he was in a position to say, "That's all right, but what about that jam tart you stole from the larder yesterday?" or something of that sort.

It would be rather nervous work living in a school of that kind, wouldn't it? But then, that was quite different; St. John Bosco looked after a lot of ragged boys from the slums, and all foreigners at that, so that they did a lot of mean and beastly things, not at all like us; they used to tell lies, for example . . . (It's very curious, isn't it, how we all think we don't tell lies? The teacher suggests we may have been copying from some book or other, and we say, "No, Sir", and he looks at us rather inquisitively and says he wishes he felt sure of that. What do we do? Draw ourselves up to our full height, and say, "Are you doubting my word, Sir?" And then Saturday night comes along, and Saturday night means, "I've told six lies, and that's all, Father." Yes, that's all. It's a dreary subject.)

Of course, if you were sitting in front of me, I could *pretend* that I knew all about your sins. If I were one of these really seasoned retreat fathers, I could get you all worked up by that business of pointing, which never fails to impress. If there were a boy standing in front of that door, I should point at him quite suddenly, and shout out, "What were YOU doing last Tuesday evening?" And all the rest of you would kick one another's shins and say "By Jove, he's got something on Whatshisname", and a pleasant time would be had by all. But, you are not here, and anyhow, I'm no good at that kind of thing; so I must be content to give you a kind of blue-print about what sin means in general, and ask you as you read to apply it to your own personal sins as if I were talking about them in particular.

Mind you, I think some of you are too keen about sin!
What I mean is, you ask me in the confessional whether
doing such and such a thing is a sin; as if you only wanted
assurance that it wasn't a sin, or not a very grave sin anyhow,
and then you would go straight off and do it. I think that is
a miserable way of treating Almighty God. Why can't you
examine your own consciences and ask yourselves whether,
on the whole, it's a good thing to do or not? Putting down
the right answer to the sum in a hasty scribble after the
teacher has told you what it is; is that a mean thing to do?
Then for God's sake don't do it. Hiding somebody else's
hairbrushes up the chimney; is that a stupidly unkind thing
to do? Then for God's sake don't do it. Grabbing the cakes
before other people can get at them; is that a hoggishly
greedy thing to do? Then for God's sake don't do it.

Whether it's some small matter like one of those, or
some larger one, the principle is the same. Don't come to
the priest and ask him to tell you it isn't a sin, or isn't a very
grave sin, as if that made it any less mean, less unkind, or
less greedy. I say, "For God's sake", and I mean it. God
doesn't want you to spend your whole life elaborately avoiding sins; he wants you to spend your life imitating our Lord
Jesus Christ. What would you think of a soldier who came
up to his superior officer in the middle of a battle, and
saluting smartly, asked whether it would be against military
regulations if he ran away? That's your spirit. The curse of
the Catholic Church is want of generosity; always brooding
about sin, instead of setting out to find what God's will is,
and doing it.

Don't let us tell one another that we save our souls by
avoiding sin. That is putting the thing all wrong, isn't it?
I mean, if somebody asks, "Did you have a nice walk?"
you don't answer, "Yes, thank you; I avoided the traffic

quite successfully." But we will always talk about the Christian life as if it consisted merely in dodging sin, a great motor-bus which sweeps round the corner and knocks you over if you are not careful! Well, of course, it's safety first, and we ought always to look both ways before we take any decision, even of moderate importance. But it's ridiculous to talk as if that were the *whole* of our Christian business. The point of the Christian life is to do at every moment the thing you think God wants you to do. If a man spent his whole life always doing what he thought God wanted him to do—though of course he would often get it wrong—he would go straight to heaven. You couldn't keep him out; couldn't. You might as well try to stop a cyclone. That is the *positive* thing that is happening all over the world—people trying to do God's will. Sin is only the back-wash of that current, only the dust of that conflict. Sin is what happens when men weary of doing God's will, and out of mere weariness enthrone something else as the motive and the master of their actions, instead of God.

All the same, there is plenty of it. And how close, all the time, to one's elbow! We get worried over it, and ask ourselves how such a state of things is possible. What is the meaning of it, we ask, this thing which all men hate, yet all men love? If we put it like that, of course, we are only indulging in a rather foolish paradox. People don't love their *sins*. The thief doesn't love theft, he loves money, or the things which money will buy. The drunkard doesn't love drunkenness, he loves drink; or that release from the dullness of his own thoughts which drink brings with it. No, we don't love our sins; sin as a rule means taking the first thing that comes to hand, means taking the line of least resistance.

Not always, of course; you couldn't say that a cat burglar

takes the first thing that comes to hand, or that the man who
robs a safe takes the line of least resistance. But usually—
think of that lie you told the other day, to get out of a
scrape; it was the first thing that came to hand, wasn't it?
You thought of it before you thought of telling the truth.
That taunt you hurled at somebody who was, for the moment,
unpopular; it was the line of least resistance, wasn't it?
You found it easier to join in, and do what everybody else
was doing, than it would have been to say, "Oh, shut up,
can't you?"

Yes, it's all nonsense to talk as if there were something
very mysterious about the sight of a human being wanting
to do one thing and doing the very opposite. It's a perfectly
common experience, even where there are no moral issues
concerned. You are lying in an arm-chair, wanting to get
up and shut the window, because there is a beastly draught,
but you don't. The long-term policy of your mind is to shut
the window, the short-term policy is to stay put; and the
short-term policy wins. And when there *are* moral issues
concerned, that is the nature of our sinning, if sin we do;
the long-term policy is to do God's will all the time, the
short-term policy is to seize this opportunity here and now,
of self-indulgence, of spiteful revenge, of unjust advantage,
whatever it may be; and the short-term policy wins. In a
way, it's so natural. To us poor human creatures the passing
moment seems always the real thing; only when we look
back on it do we see that it was nothing.

Very well, then, we've got it all taped, haven't we? Sin
is something that seems attractive, just at the moment;
looking back on it, looking forward to it, from a distance,
it has no real attraction for us whatever. . . . Well, if that's
so, why on earth am I sitting here saying all this to you?
It's a sheer waste of time. A week hence, somebody will call

you by a name you don't like, and you will go for him and do your best to knock his front teeth out. "If you could be on the spot then," you suggest, "and say a few words to me about the sin of anger, it might do some good. I'm not sure that it would do much, but it might do some. But it's no good," you go on, "talking to me about the sin of anger *now*. I know I'm a bit hot-tempered, and I don't approve of myself for it. Everything you can tell me about the sin of anger is something I've heard lots of times from my confessor, and I couldn't agree with you more. So you're wasting your breath *now*. Whereas next week you won't be there, and gosh won't I go for the little beast!"

Yes, but then I think there's something else we've got to take into account. Although in theory, on paper, you admit that you are hot-tempered and wish, quite honestly wish, that you weren't, nevertheless at the back of your mind, at the very back of your mind, you rather approve of yourself for being the kind of person who, now and again, sees red. There was something you said just now which rather seemed to indicate it. And I think if we could see into the very back of our minds we should all find that we were a bit like that. We do really think that we are rather fine fellows, sins and all. Tucked away at the back of your mind is an image which you secretly worship; it's all hidden away and swathed round with rags of pretence, but it's an image none the less, and you worship it none the less. And it's yourself. It's the self which hits out when you are annoyed, the self which stretches out to get a good share of anything that's going, the self which shrinks from any kind of discomfort, and is ready to avoid it by any means, fair or foul. Sins and all, you worship it.

Now, for heaven's sake let us have no scruples about this. What I'm saying now has nothing *whatever* to do with the purpose of amendment which you make when you go to confession. What happens when you make an act of contrition is that your will gets up and reads the Riot Act to all these faults of character which are the enemies of your peace, the bad temper, the self-conceit, the idleness, the unhealthy curiosity, and all the rest of them. And they disperse; they really do, there and then, disperse. The fact that trouble breaks out later on doesn't mean that your purpose of amendment has not been well and truly made, there and then.

But all the same, when the Riot Act has been read and the unruly demonstrators have returned to their quarters, there still remains in the very citadel of your soul this Fifth Column of which we have been speaking; this secret worship of yourself, sins and all, which goes on all the time without your knowing it, without your being conscious of it. And what I am trying to do now is to dig right down, deep down, into the inside of you and fish out this horrible great idol of self which is there, and debunk it. It isn't at all an easy thing to do, and probably I shan't make much of a success of it, but we can try.

Now, I'm not going to try and do that by shewing you more clearly, if you needed to have it shewn you more clearly, that sin is an offence against God. That, as we know, is the essential thing about it; is *the* reason why we should be sorry for it. But that conviction is more likely to come to you from some other meditation, from thinking about the Passion, from thinking about hell, than from any direct, frontal attack. The reason for that, I suppose, is that you and I can't really see sin as God sees it. If the choir sings a false note, a person like me who is pretty well tone-deaf doesn't hear there's anything wrong. He only sees the sick look on the choirmaster's face and knows that there must be something wrong. You must be musical to mind the false note; and you must be God himself, or someone very close to God, if you are to mind sin in the way God minds it. We aren't musical enough; let us try and see if there isn't any other line we can get on sin which will make it more intelligible to us, so limited, so imperfect as we are.

The sort of point I want to put to you, is that every time you commit sin you are trying to push your nature out of shape. I've no doubt that seems to you a rather moderate tone to adopt towards our sins, after all we have been saying. But it doesn't do any harm, sometimes, taking a moderate tone like that.

I expect you all have very good chests-of-drawers here; nice, old-fashioned pieces of furniture in which every drawer slides effortlessly in and out, so that you can shut it with a kick. But you know what it's like staying in a house where the drawers only just fit, so that when you try to shut a drawer it squeaks? That squeak of the drawer, when you are trying to push it in crooked, is like your conscience when your are tempted to commit a sin. Your conscience gives a squeak, doesn't it? That's because you aren't pushing in the right direction; your line of action isn't true. You see, in spite of the Fall, which has weakened it, our nature has the right instincts, and whenever we aren't doing the will of God, we contradict those instincts. In Shropshire, after a long drought, they used to say, "There's no nature in the grass"; and when the sanctuary lamp wouldn't burn properly I remember a man giving the explanation: "The oil's lost its nature; that's what it is."

A soul in mortal sin has lost its nature; it's not doing the thing it was made for, loving God; it's like lamp-oil that won't burn. Even when we commit venial sin, we impoverish our nature, like rank grass that is no real use as cattle-feed. Every act of sin is pushing crooked, is trying to force our nature in a direction in which it doesn't really want to go. Every habit of sin is an impoverishment of our nature, disqualifying it for the ends it was meant to serve. That's what I want you to see, that's what I want you to hold on to. When we aren't trying to do God's will, we are (so to speak) pushing all the time at a door marked PULL, pulling at a door marked PUSH, and you know how silly people look doing that. We forget about it, because we grow accustomed to sinning, but always there is that faint protest of conscience, like a squeak in the furniture, to shew you that your action is not *true*; you are trying to force your nature into a false pattern, to do violence to the order of your being.

I've said all that, just to make it plain that things aren't wrong simply because God tells us not to do them. He doesn't arbitrarily say, "This shall be right" and "This shall be wrong" simply to make life more difficult for us; no, he forbids us to behave in such and such a way because it is, and he knows that it is, a false pattern for us. But when we've said all that, let us remind ourselves again that the real malice of every human sin is the fact of rebellion against his commandments.

And it's here that I want to make a distinction which I think is very important. When you are being tempted, when your sin is still something that lies in the future, then (as I say) you will do well to say to yourself, "No, I can't do that; it would be a false pattern—it wouldn't really be me. I mustn't be untrue to my own nature." But when you examine your conscience and look back upon your sins, then forget all that; remind yourself, instead, that yours is a *fallen* nature, and that your sin was, in a sense, only something to be expected; be sorry for it, but don't be surprised at it. If you find yourself saying, on a Saturday night, "How *could* I have behaved like that? How *could* I be so false to my own nature?" you will get it all wrong. You will be annoyed with yourself for not having done better, for having brought down your average; and your contrition for sin will be all mixed up with personal pride. No, when you are repenting of your sins, tell God that you are sorry, but not that you are surprised. "Dear Lord, I've let you down again; how like me that was, how entirely like me that was! Dear Lord, do please make me into something worth having!" And don't doubt that he can, or that he will; even if you have made a mess of your whole life, and are lying on your death-bed, your true nature is still there underneath, only waiting for him to purge and to restore it.

9 Our Own Sins

I WANT to say a little about your sins, by way of preparation for your confession. I'm not going to talk about the malice of sin, or the importance of it. Because after all the only way in which we can form any idea of what sin means is to consider what sin cost. It cost the cruel death, with every circumstance of suffering, of an innocent victim who was, personally, God. So I only want to talk about it from a quite practical point of view, and to examine what our practical attitude ought to be, first of all towards our sins that lie in the past, the ones we are mentioning in confession, and then towards the sins which we are afraid we may be going to commit before we go to confession next.

First of all about our past sins, and our attitude towards them. How can I have been such a fool (we ask ourselves), how can I have made such a beast of myself, been so altogether unlike myself, as to do this and that, as to go on, time after time, doing this and that? As if, you see, you were rather a fine fellow really, and your sin was a kind of unaccountable lapse.

Now, that's absolutely wrong. What is quite certain, whether as a matter of theology or as a matter of experience, is that we are fallen creatures, and therefore constantly liable to give way before the assaults of temptation. In practice, we always tend to forget that; we say to ourselves, "What an extraordinary thing! I saw, quite clearly, what was the right thing to do upon such and such an occasion, and I went and did the wrong thing instead!" Yes, but you see, it isn't extraordinary in the least, once you admit the doctrine of the Fall. I dare say some of you know the odd feeling of getting out of bed for the first time in a fortnight? You're feeling perfectly all right, full of beans, and you take one step across the room to have a look in the looking-glass, and then quite suddenly you are on the floor, and in all probability have knocked over the water-jug while you were about it. You were weaker than you knew, weaker than you felt; that was the trouble. And that is the trouble with us all the time as far as our wills are concerned; we always feel such fine fellows that we forget our wills are fallen wills; and then— before we know where we are, almost, we have consented to some humiliating sin.

I should like to return to something I said in the previous chapter. When we confess our sins we must be sorry for them, we must be ashamed of them, we must hate them; but we mustn't be surprised at them. We mustn't say, "How unlike me to do a thing of that sort!" On the contrary, it was just like us to do that, fallen creatures that we are. And above all we mustn't get angry with ourselves over our sins; that never did anybody any good. You see, it's really a kind of vanity that makes us feel like that about them; we tend, unconsciously, to think of our spiritual progress as if it were like reducing a handicap at golf, or creating a record of some kind; and it makes us feel mad with ourselves that we should have let down our average in this way. We feel humiliated; but, you know, God doesn't want us to feel humiliated, he wants us to feel humbled. And that's a very different thing.

A man running after his hat in a strong wind feels humil-

iated, especially if there are a lot of people about, but
probably he doesn't feel humbled; he is full of injured pride
instead. So do let us get that clear about our sins; we are
not to be surprised at ourselves, not to be angry with ourselves; we are to say, "There, how like me to do that! Fallen
creature that I am, how absolutely dependent I am on God's
grace; how far I am, even with all the graces he has given
me, from being what he wants me to be! My God, I can do
nothing without you!" There was a French priest who wrote
a whole book called *The Art of Utilizing One's Faults*. And
that was the chief advantage he claimed for one's faults, that
if you only treat them in the right way they at least keep
you humble.

Don't mistake what I've been saying; don't run away with
the impression that, because you are a fallen creature, you
couldn't *help* consenting to sin. We are—you don't need to
have it pointed out to you—responsible for our actions. To
be sure, it isn't always possible for us to say whether a
particular fault is a sin or an imperfection, whether a particular sin we have committed, is, in the circumstances, a
mortal sin or not. In the last resort, we must leave judgment
about that in God's hands. But although in certain circumstances the weakness of our fallen nature may make it
doubtful whether we have sinned mortally or not, that isn't
always so. I am talking now of cases where you are certain
that you have sinned, where you are certain that you have
sinned mortally; and I say that even here you mustn't forget
the fall of man. It doesn't *excuse* your fault; but it *explains*
your fault; and it should help to put you in the right dispositions about it. Be patient over your own sins, as you
would be patient with the faults of another; hope, and pray,
steadily for better things. Be humble over your faults, as
you would wish to be humble over your virtues; don't add sin

to sin by treating them as if they were something unexpected.

In retreat, it's a great thing to be honest with ourselves. We should dig down and see ourselves exactly as we are— so far as that is possible; of course we can never see ourselves really straight. One thing we are tempted to do, which sometimes makes that honesty hard to achieve. We are tempted to dramatize the situation, to indulge in long rhetorical exercises to ourselves about how wicked we are, to wave our arms about and carry on as if we were terribly sorry for our sins, when in fact we aren't. Of course, very holy people like St. Theresa do contrive, somehow, to get a genuine feeling of grovelling contrition out of a record of early sins which, as far as we can see, weren't really sins at all. That's all right; they are holy people, and their consciences are altogether more sensitive than ordinary Christian consciences. But with you and me, as I say, something tends to happen which is a parody of that; a sort of hysterical outburst which doesn't rest upon any careful examination of conscience, and therefore doesn't humiliate us. ·

I can't remember where I read a poem, or who wrote it, in which somebody is represented as confessing that he is the greatest of all sinners on earth, and his guardian angel comes to him and says, "Vanity, my little man; you're nothing of the sort." I think somehow it is a useful phrase to remember. When a saint describes himself as the chief of sinners, it isn't objectively true; there are innumerable worse people in the world. But it is subjectively true, because there is, maybe, nobody else in the world who is so conscious of sin as he is. Just so a great painter, who has done a portrait of the woman he loves, may be deafened with applause by all the critics; but he shakes his head sadly, and tells them it isn't the least bit like her. He knows and they don't. That's not our position, when we say we are the chief of sinners.

Vanity may be a harsh term for it. We try to work ourselves up into an emotional state which can be described as sorrow for our sins, when there isn't really any conviction in our minds to back it.

When we do try to look at our sins coolly, honestly, and see them as they are, what gets us down sometimes is not the greatness of them so much as the littleness of them; they are so paltry, so mean. We aren't the sort of rollicking medieval Christian who killed a man and then went off on a pilgrimage to the Holy Land and spent the rest of his life in sackcloth and ashes. We seem to pass our time like coral-insects, laboriously building up for themselves a great mountain of purgatory out of tiny little peccadilloes; a harsh word here, an uncharitable criticism there, petty dishonesties, almost imperceptible self-indulgence. It humilitates us somehow, to feel that we are such mediocre people, even about our sins. It's not, of course, that we would like to be more sinful than we are; only we have the feeling that we might repent better if we had more to repent of. "Though your sins be as scarlet," Isaias says, "they shall be white as snow" —yes, that is splendid; but what is ever going to rid us of this prevailing tinge of pink?

It isn't, you see, as if these venial sins of ours represented a kind of conscious moderation on our part. We don't sit down and think, "Now, shall I poison that woman?," and then, in an access of kindliness, say to ourselves, "No, I'll write her a really bitter, a really nasty letter instead." We don't say, "Shall I rob the bank? No, not just now, but I'll put a bone button in the Sunday collection." The reason why our sins are small sins is not, as a rule, because we are good Christians, but because we are small natures. Our vices contradict one another; we don't write the unpleasant letter —because we are too idle to put it down on paper; we don't put the bone button in the collection—for fear that the other people in the pew should catch us at it. From many sins which others commit, we are preserved by force of circumstances or temperament. We aren't poor, like the people who take to burgling; we aren't passionate, like the people who make a wreck of their lives through some guilty romance. No, our whole lives move on a common, humdrum level, and they are full of common, humdrum sins. We feel like the man called Tomlinson in that poem of Kipling's, who finds himself homeless for all eternity because he's never done anything sufficiently on the heroic scale either to merit heaven, or to incur the sentence of hell.

What are we to do about it? How are we to find, in the uninspiring record of our daily faults, material for contrition on the grand scale? I think we shall do well, some of us, to review our past actions, not so much in themselves as in the tendencies they represent. You haven't done much harm in your passage through life—no. There aren't many incidents in your career which make you blush deeply when you refer to them in a general confession; well and good. But how much harm *would* you have done, if you had been in a position to do it? What kind of a mess *would* you have made of your life, if your temperament had been other than it is? Let us try to imagine that, and see if the thought of it does not, after all, drive us to our knees.

So much for our sins that are past; please God they will remain buried in the past. And now about the future; about the sins we are afraid we shall commit later on, in spite of all our contrition, in spite of all our good resolutions. You know, I think we are apt to make a mistake about good resolutions; we imagine that if we screw up our wills for a moment into a particular attitude of not-wanting-to-sin, it will have a mysterious efficacy against the temptation which

will come our way today fortnight. That, you see, is a mistake. I expect some of you know the old story of the man
who found that some of his clothes had got eaten by moths;
and he asked a friend what he ought to do to prevent that
sort of thing happening, and the friend told him to go and
buy some moth-balls; you know, those white camphor pills
you find lying about in a drawer sometimes, making your
clothes smell pretty nasty for a day or two. So he went to
the chemist's and bought some; and the next day he came
back again. The chemist was rather surprised, but he didn't
want to put off a good customer; so he said, "I'm glad you
find them effective against the moths, Sir." And the man
said, "Oh, I expect they're all right, but I haven't had enough
practice with them yet; so far, I've missed the little blighters
every time." Well, I know that's an absurd story; but it does
really give you some idea of the mistake we make if we
think we are going to make a direct attack on our sins by any
effort of our human wills. Let's think a little more about
what sin is, to make that clear.

When I spoke just now of our nature being corrupt, I
didn't mean that, since the Fall, our human nature, with all
its affections, emotions, passions and so on is something
evil, something which God hates. That is not Catholic doctrine at all; it is the mistake of the early Protestants; it is
the mistake of the Jansenists. The Fall vitiates and impairs
our human nature; but it remains something good, something beautiful, something which God loves. He didn't destroy his own handiwork because of our rebellion. No,
human nature since the Fall is not an evil thing; it is a good
thing gone wrong. All its instincts, passions, affections,
emotions are something good in themselves; but there's a
want of balance, a want of proportion between the different
elements in our make-up; our lives are not ordered by reason,

and so there is an ugly disharmony about them. To put it more simply, sin is to the soul what disease is to the body. A body which is suffering from a disease, even though it be a dangerous or a disfiguring disease, is not something evil. It is a good thing gone wrong; the disease consists in a want of proportion about it; too much uric acid or too few vitamins or whatever it may be, the kind of thing you read about in the advertisements.

And when a doctor tries to cure you of a disease by giving you medicine, he is not necessarily attacking the disease directly, but helping your body to reassert itself against the invading germs, by strengthening its powers of resistance in this direction or that. And it's the same, surely, when we are trying to get rid of sinful habits in our lives. The point is, not to attack the sinful habits directly; how can we? Sin isn't a thing you can take out with a pair of tweezers, like a splinter in your hand; it's a diseased condition of your spiritual system. And in order that sin may be eliminated from your spiritual system, your spiritual system—just like your body when it is ill—must be braced up, reinforced, provided with more powers of resistance. What does that in the first instance, I need hardly say, is divine grace. And in our efforts to co-operate with divine grace we ought, surely, to follow the same method; we ought to aim at producing good habits in our lives which will so strengthen our spiritual powers of resistance that the bad habits will be automatically driven out.

If you will pay careful attention to the needs of your soul, you will often find it possible to do that in detail. For instance, a great many of our sinful habits spring from idleness; our time has got to be wasted somehow, we feel at a loose end, and so we hang about and indulge in uncharitable conversation, or nasty, dirty conversation, or we read suggestive books, or something of that kind. Well, it's quite obvious what prescription we ought to adopt if that diagnosis is the correct one. We want to fill up our time with some honest business, some useful work, or at the least some innocent hobby; fill in the vacuum, and the sinful habit gets crowded out. Or again, a habit of grousing and complaining about things is probably due to selfishness; pay more attention to the needs of people round you, the difficulties of people round you, and the habit of grousing disappears. Or the irreverence of which you are sometimes guilty by talking and laughing in church may be dealt with in the same way. You won't get much further if you just register a resolution not to talk or laugh in church; you'll find you're doing it again before Pentecost. But resolve to get to understand the liturgy better, to follow it more intelligently, and you drive out the bad habit with the good one. You see what I'm getting at—when you make a resolution, always try if possible to resolve on something positive, not merely something negative. I've only given you these examples as examples; what I want you to do in order to carry out the suggestion is to go to your confessor some time, or to any priest in whom you have confidence, and ask him what is the best way of tackling this or that difficulty.

But best of all, better than any other good you can hope to acquire, is the habit of cultivating the presence of God in your daily life. I've tried to suggest already what I mean by that. I mean pulling yourself up at odd moments during the day—when you are just switching over from one occupation to another, when you come in from a game and sit down for a minute or two before changing, when you're waiting about for an appointment; odd moments, not fixed times—pulling yourself up just in those few seconds while your mind is unoccupied, and letting it dwell on the thought of God. God, not far away somewhere in the clouds, but close to you all the time, his Spirit enfolding and embracing your spirit, closer than hands or feet. No need to utter any vocal prayers, no need even to make any act or form any aspiration with your will, just let your mind rest, for a moment, on the thought of him. Don't wait till the hour of temptation comes, and betake yourself, then, to panic-stricken prayer; make a practice of living, as far as possible, in his presence; and then you will begin to find the bad habits falling away; even those which seemed most intimate to you, most difficult to get rid of.

The time you spend in examining your own consciences, if you spend it wisely, will do you more good than any advice you get from me. So I will only leave you with those two thoughts. Hate your old sins and be sorry for them, but be humble over them, and don't get impatient with yourself over them. Make plans for the future, not by asking yourself what bad habits you ought to avoid, but by asking yourself what good habits you ought to cultivate.

10 Sins of the Tongue

I'VE heard a story—I wish I knew whether all the stories I hear are true—about a lady who was standing on a railway platform and got a piece of grit in her eye from a passing train. I dare say she had a looking-glass in her bag, because for some reason people do seem to carry looking-glasses about with them; but for some reason she couldn't get the grit out, and it was particularly painful. So she went to the nearest porter and asked him if he could get it out for her. And he said, "All right; stand quite still, mum"; and then he put his face quite close to hers, as if to see the piece of grit better, and quite suddenly he shot out his tongue and licked it out before she knew what was happening.

There are all sorts of morals to that story; one is, to shew you what is the best way to take grit out of your eye; though of course it's not a remedy you can apply very easily yourself unless you have an unusually large tongue. But the moral I want to draw from it is, what an extraordinarily delicate piece of mechanism the human tongue is—or any tongue for that matter; iguanas (I think it is) can catch flies with their tongues, which is more than you can do. This extraordinary piece of mechanism which you can use for sticking on a postage-stamp or finding out whether your food is nice or playing a penny whistle, which you can put out at the doctor when you're ill or at other people when

4*

you are in a bad temper; it would be an awful thing not
to have a tongue, wouldn't it? And then, on the top of all
that, the human race has discovered a way of waggling its
tongue about so as to make noises, and noises which mean
something, as I'm doing now.

Since the tongue is such a very adaptable instrument, it's
perhaps not surprising that when we think about our sins,
we class a whole set of them as sins of the tongue. We don't
really include under that heading all the sins over which our
tongue comes in useful. If you were to lick the cream off the
top of the trifle before anybody else could get at it, that
would be a sin of the tongue, but it wouldn't be useful to
mention it in that way in confession. No, we ordinarily
confine that term to sins by which we abuse the gift of speech.

Even so, you know, it's rather bad luck to throw all the
blame on our poor old tongues. We don't do it with other
parts of the body; if somebody worships in front of a heathen
idol, for example, we don't describe that as a sin of the knee.
And, by the way, while I'm on that subject, will you examine
your conscience for a moment—which leg do you genuflect
with? The right leg? Or the left leg? Or the right leg when
you're sitting on the right-hand side of the chapel, and the
left when you're sitting on the left? Because, unless you
have got something permanently wrong with your right leg,
that is the only leg on which the Catholic Church expects
you to genuflect, ever. I don't want you to mention it in
confession, as a sin of the knee, if you have genuflected on
the left leg; it isn't a sin, it's just a mistake. Like that story
of the lady who said in confession that she was afraid when
she looked in the looking-glass she sometimes admired her
own appearance, and the priest said, "My child, you are here
to confess your sins, not your mistakes."

Well, I'm afraid we are rather getting off the subject.

What I want to talk to you about, as I dare say you have guessed by this time, is sins of the tongue. I tried to find out whether there wasn't a list of them anywhere: because, as I dare say you've noticed, Catholic theology is as a rule very keen on drawing up lists of things. But I can't find that there is one, so I thought we would make up a list for ourselves. This one, I think, will do. First, swearing; then, lying; then, quarrelling; then, flattering; then, crabbing or carping; then, grousing or complaining; and lastly, boasting. That makes seven, and seven always seems to be the right number to aim at.

Swearing is one of those sins which certain classes of the community indulge in more than others. People talk about swearing like a bargee; I don't know why, because whenever I've been out in a boat on canals or navigable rivers I've always found the people on barges very calm and placid. But anyhow, it's not a sin to which most of you are much addicted.

There are just three things to be said about swearing, though. One is this; it's not so much a sin of the tongue as a sin of the temper. Now, it's true that different people have different tempers; that is what the word means; and one person naturally flares up much more easily than another. But it is part of the business of the soul to get your temper more under control; and those swear-words are a kind of barometer which registers your success; if the barometer registers VERY STORMY, that means you ought to be taking yourself in hand a bit. Another thing is this; swearing shocks people, sometimes, whom you wouldn't expect to be shocked; take a look round at your company before you let fly. And the third is this; if you find the name of God frequently crossing your lips when you don't mean it to, that shews that the thought of God has been driven down into your sub-consciousness (which is where the swear-words come from); and that means that the thought of God is not in the foreground of your mind. Is that as it should be? If we really tried harder to live in the presence of God, we couldn't take his name in vain like that; it would be something too solemn, too precious, for that.

And then about lying, which includes perjury. The main point I want to make is this; that if you develop a habit of exaggerating things or misrepresenting things, you very quickly build up for yourself a reputation for insincerity; people don't attach any importance to your opinion, and all their relations with you become difficult because they know they can't quite trust you. Try always, in the first place, to see things straight in your own mind—the lie comes from the mind, not from the tongue; don't let prejudices dim your outlook, don't borrow other people's opinions without examining them, don't talk just for the sake of talking. Otherwise, your own mind will begin to see crooked; and if that happens, you won't be *able* to tell the truth; the truth won't be in you. Before I took to wearing spectacles, I always used to think that my short-sighted friends wasted a great deal of their lives in polishing their spectacles. I know now how easily one's spectacles get clouded over, and what a lot of polishing they take. Well, it's the same, if you see what I mean, with your mental outlook. It will get all furred over, and see the world crooked, if you aren't constantly polishing it, so to speak, by testing your opinions, by sifting in your own mind the views you hear expressed in common talk, by being on your guard when you read, and especially when you read the newspapers, with the reflection that probably a great deal of this isn't true.

Then the next sin I've called quarrelling; oddly enough there's no word that covers it all. It includes losing your temper and saying things which are intended to wound people, it includes nagging—I wonder why we call it nagging? It has nothing to do with horses. I mean going on and on reminding people of some foolish thing they said or did, of some habit in them which you dislike. It includes teasing, which is different because you do it for your own fun, or to amuse the company. Any of these things may do more or less harm, according to the sensitiveness or insensitiveness of your victim. This is a good thing to remember, that most people are rather more sensitive than they appear to be, rather more sensitive than they let on to be. You say of a friend, "Oh, she's awfully sweet; she never minds what you say about her; she can take any amount of chaff." But it isn't necessarily true; some people feel these things much more deeply than you know, and cry about them afterwards. That applies, you see, even to teasing, when you probably don't mean any harm.

Obviously it's worse when you say things with the intention of wounding; our Lord treats it in the Sermon on the Mount, if you remember, as a kind of murder, when you say to a person "Thou fool", or even "Raca", which I suppose would be about the same as saying, "You silly ass". What I would like to suggest here, is this. If you are talking, tête à tête, to somebody who has annoyed you, or gets on your nerves, and find that you are being rather bright about inventing unpleasant things to say to him, just stop for a moment and imagine that you are a third person sitting in the room and listening to the conversation. There's something particularly horrible, don't you think, about sitting by when somebody has lost his temper and is saying really mean and spiteful things? Well, try to listen to yourself speaking *as if you were a third person in the room,* and learn to judge yourself by that standard. And ask God for the grace to shut up.

The next sin on our list is flattering. I really put that in because, if I remember right, Dante gives the flatterers a whole circle of their own in hell, which shews that in the Middle Ages anyhow flattery went on, and that it was considered a bad thing.

I think it's probably true to say that flattery is not a sin to which you are greatly tempted, while you are at school. If anything it is the other way round; some of you are almost too keenly alive to the duty of fraternal correction. At the same time I seem to remember phrases one used at school which weren't wholly remote from the idea of flattery. One used to talk, I mean, of sucking up to a person, or buttering him up, when one wanted to get something out of him. I wonder whether there aren't, perhaps, equivalent phrases in use today. Don't ever praise people falsely to their faces. Don't praise people to their faces, fulsomely, even when the praise you bestow on them is quite true, unless you feel certain in the first place that you have no ulterior motive for doing it, and in the second place that you aren't simply joining in, out of human respect, in a chorus of admiration for someone who happens to be popular, at the risk of turning his head and making him conceited. I am speaking now in the interests of our own sex; which gets a lot more flattery from the other sex than is good for it. Try and see things straight, I have already told you that; try also to see *people* straight—don't get taken in by surface charm, and by bogus reputations.

And now, it's time we went on to Sin number Five, which is much more serious. I have called it crabbing or carping;— though it has nothing to do with either of the fish in question. A fish, being dumb, can hardly set us a bad example in connection with sins of the tongue, can it? It would be a good thing for many of us if we were more like fish. At the same time, the uncanny sideways motions of a crab do, perhaps, give you some idea of the character I want to talk to you about now; the character of the person who is always saying unpleasant things about people behind their backs. They are not always the same people who say unpleasant things to one's face; on the contrary, it is not uncommon to find people who flatter you to your face, and then say beastly things about you behind your back. Wherever people live herded together, as in a boarding school, you will always find sins against charity of this kind. Wherever people live herded together, sins against charity of this kind do continual harm, poison the atmosphere of the life you live in common, give rise to uneasiness and suspicion. Let me just shew you how it does harm to the person who talks scandal, the person to whom the scandal is talked, and the person about whom the scandal is talked.

It does harm to you, when you talk uncharitably. Picking holes in other people's characters gives you, by comparison, far too good an opinion of yourself; you are, by implication, contrasting yourself with them all the time. It also sours your own character, gives you a nasty, peering habit of mind, always on the look-out for the weak points in human nature. And it produces those same defects in the company before which you are talking; when scandal starts, everybody wants to join in. At the same time, it makes everybody feel uncomfortable, because it occurs to them that the same kind of gossip is going on about them the moment their backs are turned; nobody dares to leave the room, for fear they should be the next to be pulled to pieces.

And of course it does harm to the person you are talking about. True or false. It does, of course, matter whether the scandal you repeat is true or false; if it is false, for example, and if it is a grave charge you have brought, then you are bound to make restitution by undeceiving those whom you have misled. But scandal is scandal, whether it's something you know to be true or something you know to be false, or, as more often happens, something you think may be true but aren't a bit sure. The point is that you have belittled somebody's stature in the eyes of his fellow-creatures, have left him to go through the world with a black mark against him. Even mimicking people behind their backs can do such a lot of harm. If you heard, next day, that he was dead, you'd be miserable about having talked like that. If he was terribly ill, or upset by bad news from home, you would be taking back all you had said, and trying to make amends, out of pity for him. That shews what you really think; that shews, you know, really, you are being a mean little beast when you talk uncharitably. But you go on.

And then complaining or grousing—there again, I don't know what the unfortunate bird has done, to be connected with this irritating habit. It lives in very cold places and feeds on heather, but it never seems to complain. We have, on the whole, a very good time, and we complain like mad. Now, I'm not asking you to do an easy thing when I ask you not to grumble. It's something, heaven knows, which comes natural to mankind, and it does bring one a slight relief in times of discomfort to be able to let off steam about it—if you will pardon a vulgar comparison, it has rather the same effect as scratching a midge-bite. All the same, it does lower the general tone, does spoil the sweetness, of life in a community, if people are always going round exchanging grievances and telling each other something ought to be done about it. God expects sacrifices from all of us; and he values that offering most when we bear our discomforts without mentioning them. Mortification is a precious balm which loses its scent if we are always taking the lid off the jar.

And there was one other thing—oh yes, boasting. This is a much nicer sin than any of the others we've been talking about; a good healthy sort of sin by comparison. Of course, we don't boast directly; it would be awfully bad form to say, "Gosh, I did play tennis well this afternoon." But if you watch yourself, you will find there are a lot of ways in which you can boast indirectly. You can tell your partner how well she played, hoping she will say, "Not nearly as well as you.' You can monopolize the conversation when other people wa it to talk. You can try to cap every story you hear with the tory of something much more remarkable which happened to you or to a friend of yours, like the man from Scotland wher they shewed him the falls of Niagara, and asked him if he didn't think that remarkable, and he said, "For bonny I won't say, but for queer, I know a man at Paisley's got a peacock with a wooden leg." You can talk knowingly, like one who has seen a great deal of the world, to impress other people who haven't seen so much of it. All that isn't considered bad form, but it *is* boasting, you know. As I say, it's not much of a sin, but it is after all a fault against humility; and I think when you examine your conscience it is as well to ask yourself whether you haven't talked for effect, and tried to make the conversation minister to your own vanity.

Have I used bad language? Have I told lies? Have I said nasty things *to* people? Have I flattered them for my own ends? Have I said nasty things *about* people? Have I complained? Have I thrown my weight about in conversation? There is a simple scheme, to form part of your examination of conscience.

I I *Prayer*

I HAD to go over to Dublin some years ago for the Eucharistic Congress; at these Congresses, as you probably know, Catholics from the oddest parts of the world meet and exchange experiences. I was calling on the rector of St. Francis Xavier's, the big Jesuit church there, and while I was talking to him one of the priests came and said, "Do come into the gallery and have a look; Mar Ivanios is saying Mass here." This was a bishop from the South of India; he belonged to a religious body which had been in schism since the fifth century or thereabouts, and had just joined up again with the Church, so naturally there was a certain amount of excitement about him. I met him afterwards, and he was an interesting man (the only man I have ever met, I think, who wore a collar without a shirt). I expect you know that when these Oriental people come back to the Church they don't conform to the Roman rite; they don't say Mass in Latin, for example, or observe our rubrics; they stick to their old ceremonies, which have quite as long a history in Christendom as the Roman rite, and perhaps longer.

So we all went into the tribune at the back of the church; and there was Mar Ivanios, who had more or less got to the Consecration, dressed in the most outlandish clothes, which looked to the profane eye as if they had come out of

the stage properties of the *Mikado,* turning round to face
the congregation, with the chalice in one hand and the paten
in the other, roaring. I can only describe it as roaring,
because it really didn't give you the impression of a chant
of any kind. And this, remember, was a perfectly good
Catholic Mass, only rather different from the Mass we are
accustomed to. And the thought struck me, for the church
was quite full of people, as churches always are in Dublin,
"What impression is all this making on the poor people of
Dublin? Will they look astonished, or shocked, or edified,
or what?" So I crept along to the front of the tribune, and
looked down at the congregation beneath. And there were
rows and rows of pious biddies, all with their eyes shut, just
going on with their rosaries, "Holy Mary, Mother of God,
pray for us sinners now and at the hour of our death."

That gave me a curious picture of the Catholic Church,
and the strange diversity there is in its unity. It also made me
bothered, not for the first time, over the question, "What
is it we mean when we talk about *hearing* Mass, or about
saying our prayers? What difference can it make to our
spiritual position, in time or eternity, that we should have
heard certain words said, or have said certain words ourselves? And what kind of effort ought we to make, if any,
to follow, with our minds, what the priest is saying?" I
thought I would like to give you a meditation about saying
your prayers; because after all we spend a good deal of our
lives doing it, and most of us have an uneasy suspicion that
a good deal of the time we spend on it is time wasted—is it
wasted through our fault? We don't quite know. And then
we come across that answer in the Catechism, where it says:
"Those who, at their prayers, think neither of God nor of
what they say, do not pray well, but they offend God, if
their distractions are wilful." Which makes us wonder

whether it wouldn't be a good thing to say fewer prayers, in the hope of offending God rather less.

Well, first of all let's try to get this business about wilful distractions straight in our minds. It is a wilful distraction if you deliberately do something in church which is directly calculated to distract your attention from the worship of God. If you brought a detective story into chapel and read it during Mass, that would be a wilful distraction. It is a wilful distraction if, say, you come across a phrase in a hymn which reminds you of some joke you have been enjoying with a friend, and you look round deliberately—not instinctively, but deliberately—with the intention of catching that friend's eye. It is a wilful distraction if you deliberately start doing sums in your head, or thinking out some plan for making a nuisance of yourself, with the intention of whiling away the time, because (you say to yourself) you can't be bothered to pay any attention to what is going on round you. By such deliberate distractions you offend God. You don't offend God very much. I shouldn't think he minds it nearly as much as he minds your saying something spiteful about a person you don't like. It's not really anything very surprising, at your age (if I may say so), and in your circumstances. But it is irreverence all the same.

Now suppose it's not quite like that. Suppose that, in turning over the pages of your missal, or some other pious book, you come across something which interests you, although it hasn't got anything to do with today's feast, or with the service you are attending at the moment. Suppose you catch somebody's eye without meaning to, and giggle slightly, as a suitable form of recognition. Suppose you find you have drifted off into an agreeable train of thought, making plans for the holidays or what not, and, finding your attention thus wandering, you don't make any effort to call it to order, but just let it go on. All those things are distractions, and they are semi-voluntary distractions. But you are not, I should say, offending God. These things aren't sins, they are only imperfections; and it's better that you should be in church behaving in this imperfect manner than not be in church at all.

But we have also to reckon, how much we have to reckon, with *in*voluntary distractions. There you are, with your finger on the right bead of your rosary, saying Hail Mary's in a loud and devout voice, but you are thinking about all sorts of things. You are thinking about how unjust the teacher was to you when he said what he really thought about you the last time you were in class; you are thinking about a spider that is crawling up the back of the person in front of you; you are wondering what you could do to improve your service at tennis; you are wondering whether such and such a day in the near future will be a holiday; you are thinking about almost anything, and then suddenly "Glory be to the Father and to the Son and to the Holy Ghost", and you realize with a nasty shock that you aren't quite certain which mystery you have been meditating on. You haven't done anything to invite these distractions to come your way; they just came. And that kind of thing, you say, is always happening. Well, what are we to make of it?

In the first place, don't imagine that you are the only person who is subject to distractions of this kind. You look at the girl next you, and find her looking up with a rapt expression, as if she might go off into an ecstasy at any moment; don't be taken in by that, she is probably thinking about herself too. Everybody, except a handful of saints and mystics, suffers from distractions in prayer, and suffers badly. There's no reason at all to imagine that the devil has a special down on you, and takes this opportunity of working off his spite against you; no reason to imagine that you are an interesting nervous case, and had better go and see a psychoanalyst about it in the holidays. After all, the thing stands to reason. Attention is a very difficult thing to command; I don't suppose I should be far out if I suggested that most of you have been spoken to pretty sharply, at least once this term, for having your thoughts elsewhere or "being in the moon", as some people call it, during class. There are some exciting things in life which do manage to rivet your attention, like a motor-accident in the street; and anything which has an immediate appeal to your senses, like a display of fireworks, or arouses your curiosity, like a detective story, or awakes you to a spirit of competition, like a game of chess, will do the same thing. But whenever the thing on which you are engaged, whether it be work or prayer, is something on which you have to bring your attention to bear, like making a horse face up to a fence, you will *always* find that it wants to shy and go off somewhere else. That's mere common-sense; and one of the reasons why prayer is good for us is that it does need a series of acts of the will if we are to make anything of it. God allows our minds to wander, so that from time to time we may have to make an effort—use our wills—in forcing our attention back to him.

That's the first point I want to make; and the next point is this—don't ever tell yourself that because you say such and such prayers with ridiculously little attention, therefore it is not worth while saying those prayers at all. I'm thinking now more of what you do in the holidays, and of what you'll do when you've left school, than of what you do at school; you aren't in a position there to say exactly what you will do and what you won't do, because at school things have to be done by numbers, and so you all have to

toe the line. Well, take a thing like saying grace before
and after meals. It's very hard indeed, in a fraction of time
like that, to recollect yourself and think what you're saying;
nine times out of ten, at least, the thing misses fire. All the
same, it is a thing worth doing to *say* grace; or even simply
to cross yourself if you are too flustered at the moment to
remember the words of a grace. However mechanical it
may become, it is a gesture worth making; a gesture of
recognition to the God who gives us everything we have
and everything we are. You don't need to make an enormous
business of it, like a friend of mine who was told that when
he said grace he looked like a man trying to pour treacle
into his mouth. On the other hand, you don't want to reduce
it to an extreme minimum, like a High Church don at
Oxford who was asked by one of his colleagues, "I say,
Burney, why have you given up scratching your chest?"
And don't leave it out when you go to stay with non-
Catholics; they won't think any the better of you for it. Try,
if you can, to be grateful when you say grace, but don't give
up saying it from a kind of scruple.

Then there are your morning and evening prayers; those,
too, are apt to become mechanical, partly because they are
so much the same day after day, partly because you are
liable to be a bit short of time in the morning, and a bit
sleepy in the evening. But, however distractedly you say
them, they are worth saying. The mere fact of kneeling down
and honouring God externally is some kind of tribute, however wretchedly paid, from you to him. Incidentally, this
is a good rule to observe in case you are the kind of person
who is tempted to do otherwise—don't repeat one of your
fixed prayers if you find you have said it distractedly. Ask
God's pardon, if you like, for any wilfulness there may
have been in the distraction, but don't start saying it over

and over; that leads to scruples and unhappiness. God knows the dust from which we are made, knows our weakness, and doesn't expect too much of us. At the same time we obviously ought to do all we can to avoid distraction. I mean, if you are always racing when you say your morning prayers, you are not likely to say them very well, and to avoid that, you want to be fairly smart about heaving yourself out of bed when you are called. But whatever happens, don't ever start or finish the day without offering it somehow, however hurriedly or sleepily, to God.

However, I suppose what worries us most is our distractions in church. Because after all there we are, in the presence of the Blessed Sacrament, and it feels so irreverent to be thinking about a whole lot of unimportant and undignified things. I know, but, as I've tried to explain, that can't be helped; we are not, except within very narrow limits, masters of ourselves in this way—we can't put up, as it were, a trespassers-will-be-prosecuted notice on the edge of our minds, and tell the intruding thoughts not to come in; it doesn't do any good.

Can we do anything about it? Well, perhaps just one or two things. Don't fidget, don't get into the habit of fidgeting, in church. If you suddenly realize that you are swinging your leg to and fro, or fiddling with the markers in your prayer-book, stop. I don't know what the psychologists say about fidgeting, and I probably shouldn't believe it if I did. But I can tell you this as a matter of experience, that fidgets in church are the ally of distractions in church. If you can manage to stop swinging that leg, you will find automatically, I think, that your mind comes back to the thing you want to think about, your prayer, instead of continually rushing off at odd tangents. And that will last just for the two or three minutes which pass before you find yourself swinging your leg again. And don't, more than you can help, look about you—even quite innocently, without the idea of catching anybody's eye; if you keep your eyes open, try to keep them directed towards, say, a bare patch of wall, or, of course, towards the altar itself; don't keep on looking round at different objects, even if they are holy ones.

But when we've said all that, I'm afraid we still haven't gone a very long way towards reducing the number of our distractions; we have got to make the best of them. How are we to make the best of them? The pious books tell us that there are three different kinds of attention which we can pay to God when we worship him; attention of the tongue, attention of the mind, and attention of the heart. People who are bound to say office, as I am, have got to be careful that we get through the office with our lips, even if we do nothing else. And I think I would make this rule, if I were you—always to join in in saying the rosary or any other devotion in which you are expected to take part, unless you are quite certain that it is holy thoughts which are occupying your mind. If you are really thinking, say, about our Lady's Annunciation when the first mystery of the rosary is being said, then go on thinking about it, and don't bother to join in the Hail Mary's, if you don't feel like it. But if your thoughts are wandering, at least it's a good thing to make your tongue say the words; that will be something done, anyhow.

Still, you can't do that at Mass; and Mass is I suppose the biggest part of your prayer, and certainly the most important part of your prayer. When you are hearing Mass, which is most important, to be attending with your mind or to be attending with your heart? Is it a good thing to follow in a book, and try to make out what the feast of the day is, and what on earth St. Paul meant when he wrote the

Epistle? Or is it a better thing to occupy your mind with the things you want to pray about; to make acts of love and humility in preparation for your Communion, and so on? And are you to feel bound to make such and such acts, because they are there in the pious book which your aunt gave you, or are you allowed just to let your mind dwell lovingly on the thought of God, and rest contentedly in the knowledge of our Lord's presence on the altar, his nearness to you and his great goodness to you?

If you ask me questions like that, I shall make a rather tiresome answer but one which I feel sure is the true answer: "The golden rule is that there is no golden rule." What is the best thing for you to do is the thing which is most successful in keeping away distractions. What is the best thing for you to do on this particular morning is the thing which is most successful in keeping away distractions this particular morning. Don't feel bound to follow the words of the Mass, even if the priest at home is keen on the liturgy and is always advising you to follow the words of the Mass —unless you find it helps. Don't go through those printed acts in the book even if your aunt did give you the book— unless you find it helps. Don't force yourself into a groove; keep your mind open and supple, ready to follow God's guidance from day to day. If you find, sometimes—and per- haps especially on days when you are feeling happy and in a good temper with the world—that a nice, comfortable feel- ing of being in God's presence comes flooding into your mind, hold on to that, don't let yourself be disturbed from that; it will do you more good than all the books in the world, the missal included. And the same is true whenever you feel your mind drawn towards God, in love, in sorrow for your sins, anything like that. If your mind is buzzing with distracting thoughts, bury your nose in a book as much as possible. If you are feeling tired and not up to much in the way of mental effort, let yourself go into God's hands and let him do what he will with your thoughts; just offer yourself quietly to him. Don't tie yourself down to any plan, any rule; especially over your thanksgiving after Communion —that is the time when we should be most free, most ready to respond to whatever thoughts God sends us.

And when the distractions do come? They will, of course, all the same. When the distractions do come, is there any way of fighting them? Well, I think the rule for fighting distractions is the same as the rule for fighting wasps. The best way to fight a wasp, unless it has actually settled on your nose, is to take no notice of it. If you wave your arms and flick your napkin at it, it comes back again at once, full of curiosity to know what all these odd air-pockets come from. So it is with distractions; if you try to face up to them and struggle against them; if you say to yourself, There's the Sanctus Bell, and I haven't prayed a bit! what a hopeless creature I am, kneeling in church and thinking about whatever it was, then you set all your distractions off again, you'll be thinking of whatever it was before you know where you are. No, what you want to do is to switch your mind back, quite quietly, to the business of your prayer, as if nothing had happened. Don't even make an act of contrition about it, not till Mass is over. Don't get angry with yourself, take it as quite an ordinary thing; it *is* quite an ordinary thing.

There's one other point I want to mention about prayer, and then I've done. At least, you might call it two points, but it's one really—two sides of the same medal. Don't ever think that it's wrong to ask God for quite insignificant things you happen to want. He likes, be sure of that, to share even your most undignified confidences. And at the same time, don't forget that he does want you to ask him for spiritual blessings too; for the grace to overcome some particular temptation you have, for guidance in some important decision you may have to make, for more faith, for more love, above all for the gift of final perseverance. It's quite true that God doesn't need to be told you want these things, unimportant or important; but then, prayer isn't just telling God what you want. Prayer is shewing God you trust him, trust him to look after you and everybody you are fond of, and then abandoning your will to his, assuring him that you know his will is best, and his way for you the right way. Your prayer is business-like, and has been a success, in so far as it is a test and a token of confidence between you and him.

12 _The Mass_

THERE was a boy who was given a holiday one day, I don't quite know why. It was a bright spring day, about this time of year, and, as there was a lake near where he lived, he thought he would go out in his father's boat, if his father would let him. His mother said he would drown himself; but his father said nonsense, he was quite old enough to be trusted with the boat just for one day. His mother said anyhow he would lose himself and not be home in time for supper; that kind of thing had happened before. He said, "That's all right, Mother, I swear I'll be home in time." In the end they compromised; he must take some food with him in case he got lost and felt hungry. His mother put half a dozen rolls into his satchel; he wanted fewer, because they were rather heavy to carry, but she insisted on that.

Well, he had a great time on the lake. He trawled a bit with some contraption of his own—only a home-made affair, but he was in luck that day; he managed to catch three quarter-pounders, and only just lost another. By that time—he hadn't got a watch, of course, he wasn't that kind of boy—he spotted from the position of the sun that it was getting well on into the afternoon; and he was also beginning to feel a little hungry. So he thought it would be a good idea if he put in to land—he was at the far side of the

lake now, away from home—and tried to cook his fish
for luncheon. There was a fishing-boat near where he
landed, drawn up to the shore, with nobody in it, and he
wondered idly what it was doing there, because that part
of the country was miles away from anywhere, and you
wouldn't expect to find people about. He cooked the fish
as best he could, and that wasn't very well; but he had to
pretend it was all right, because he'd cooked them himself. He ate one with a roll, and it wasn't too bad; the
other two he put back in his satchel. Then he thought he
would go and explore. He would look for the people the
other boat belonged to; perhaps they would be smugglers
or something exciting like that. There was a rough path
which went up the cliff, so it looked as if they would probably have taken that.

However, he was in for a surprise. He hadn't gone far
when he found, not just the boat's crew, but a whole crowd
of people collected; hundreds and hundreds of them, or
so he thought, all collected in a sort of hollow a little way
from the shore. As far as he could make out, somebody
was making a speech to them. It looked as if it might be
a political meeting; rather an unusual thing just then,
although he knew from his father's talk that it had been
common enough a few years before he was born. Politics
bored him anyhow, and he was rather shy with all those
people about, so he didn't obey his first instinct, which was
to squirm his way to the front and see what was happening.
No, he just sat down on the edge of the crowd and rested
there; nobody took much notice of him. He took out the
two fish he 'had left, and started weighing them roughly
in his hands; no, he considered, it would hardly be possible
to describe them as half-pounders.

A kind-faced man passed by just then, a fisherman by

the look of him, who was very interested and asked him all about them; and he said, "What a good careful mother you must have, to have made you take those rolls with you." After a time, the speech-making seemed to be at an end; and the people round him started talking, and some of them began to move off as if they were going home. Just then the man came back, and said would he very much mind giving away what he had left of his provisions? Because they were badly wanted by some people who were short of food. And, when he consented, he was taken off into the middle of the crowd; and there, very shyly, he came forward and handed over the contents of his satchel, not to the first man but to a younger Man who seemed to be a friend of his, and was in command of the whole proceedings.

"One of his disciples, Andrew, the brother of Simon Peter, saith to him, There is a boy here that hath five barley loaves and two fishes. But what are these among so many? Then Jesus said, Make the men sit down. Now there was much grass in the place. The men therefore sat down, in number about five thousand. And Jesus took the loaves, and when he had given thanks, he distributed to them that were set down. In like manner also of the fishes, as much as they would."

I wonder how long it took you to spot what the story was? I didn't begin that story from the wrong end *merely* in order to mislead you. I began it from the boy's end, because if you come to think of it he is a rather important personage in the affair. He is only mentioned by St. John; but it's interesting to wonder how the five loaves and the two fishes got there. Our Lord didn't create food out of nothing, though of course he could have. No, he was going to do a miracle, but he wanted to be supplied, by ordinary human means, with the bread and fishes that were to be

5

the basis of his miracle. And he chose that boy, who could contribute so very little; just a few rolls and some fish that probably weren't cooked very nicely—but he could contribute something; that was the point. He wants us to give the best we have, and leave his Omnipotence to deal with it.

The subject I'm leading up to, of course, is the Mass. Our Lord allowed a casual member of his audience, a young boy, a stranger, to provide him with the material requisites for his miracle in the wilderness because, I think, he wanted us to see that in the Blessed Sacrament we mustn't expect *everything* to be done for us; he does want us to provide *something* on our own behalf, though it is so little, though it is so easily provided; just common bread and a little wine. The Mass, you see, demands a kind of conspiracy between the priest on one side and the laity on the other. We are not to think of it as merely the business of the priest, who will be quite contented if he can raise a boy from somewhere to answer the responses at "his" Mass. No, the laity have a true share in the sacrifice; "Pray, brethren, that my sacrifice *and yours* may be acceptable" —it is their Mass, not just his. And when you hand the cruets to the priest, you are not just handing him something which it's too much trouble for him to take for himself. You are performing a symbolical act; presenting to him, in the name of the faithful laity, those requisites of the altar which are to be the material of a sacrifice, his sacrifice and yours. You are that boy by the lake-side in Galilee; and the priest is St. Andrew, taking from you your boyish offering and passing it on into our Lord's hands that he may do his miraculous will with it.

Ask yourself once again what it was that our Lord did in the miracle of the five thousand. Here are five barley loaves; not large ones, I imagine; there is no reason to think that the boy who had them was a baker's boy going round with a cart—probably they were quite small, and the people who sat down to the meal had been away from home for two or three days, and they were certainly hungry. Let us suppose each loaf was big enough to satisfy one mouth. Enough for five, and five thousand to be fed; that means either a sum in addition or a sum in multiplication. It would have been possible for our Lord to create, there and then, 4995 new loaves and hand them round with the others. When he was tempted in the wilderness, the devil pointed to the flat stones that were lying about there and suggested that he should turn some of those, by a miracle, into bread. He could have done that now, if he would; it was possible for him to collect 4995 stones and turn them into loaves. But he did not do so; he did not add anything to the existing stock of bread; he took what there was and multiplied it.

If you think that was a difficult thing for him to do, you must remember that it is he who multiplies the grain of wheat that falls into the ground, so that it springs up into something much greater and more abundant than itself; when he multiplied the loaves he was not really doing anything new, he was doing what he does every year, when he gives us the harvest, but he was doing it all at once, without the customary processes which intervene between seed-time and harvest—that was the miraculous part of it. The five loaves grew, in his hands, into the same quantity of bread that would have been present if there had been five thousand loaves instead of five.

I say it is a symbolical act; for the laity, in offering the bread and wine which are to become the Body and Blood of Christ, are offering also their prayers to him; their needs, their aspirations, their ambitions, their hopes to him; all *that* is to be taken up into his sacrifice, made part of his sacrifice. You must think of our Lord's Sacrifice in the Mass as a great whirlwind, which catches up your prayers, your weak human prayers, and sweeps them away in the current of its own impetuous movement; or as a great furnace, in which your prayers glow with sudden heat, like the wire filaments under an electric spark. Then you will see what it means when we talk about "going to Mass" or "hearing Mass" or "assisting at Mass". It doesn't mean, or rather it oughtn't to mean, simply hanging about in a building where Mass is going on. It means, it ought to mean, being caught up and vitalized by the spirit of our Lord's eternal Sacrifice.

And that's why I used to get so impatient when undergraduates who had been at Catholic schools told me, as they sometimes would, that they didn't understand why Mass should be compulsory at such places. One of them told me that he'd been made to go to Mass every day while he was at school, and the consequence was he was bored with the Mass. Well, he was killed in the war, as a military chaplain, so he's all right. But really, you know, "bored" with the Mass! Did he think he was coming to Mass as a kind of entertainment?

Of course you're bored, if you sit and kneel in the same place for twenty-five minutes on end not thinking of anything, not trying to think of anything, just waiting for the twenty-five minutes to be over. The presence of a man dressed up in rather expensive clothes going through a set of motions and gestures which you have seen several hundred times before isn't going to thrill you; why should it? The boredom comes from the inertia of your own mind; and your own mind is inert because you haven't begun to realize what Mass is about; what Mass is for. You have to associate yourself with the action of it by throwing yourself into the spirit of its sacrifice; if not, you will get about as much satisfaction out of it as a deaf man gets out of a concert. Oh yes, you satisfy your obligation by merely being present, if it's a Sunday or a great feast, whether you make an effort to join in or not. Just so, if you have promised to go out for a walk with a person, you keep your promise if you merely march by his side, without uttering a word the whole time. But that's not what going out for a walk means; and that's not what "going to Mass" means, or ought to mean, if we have any sense of the claim which Almighty God makes upon our faculties of worship.

You see, you join yourself with the priest in the offering he is making. And you can offer to God anything that is in your mind, unless it is something sinful—and even then you can approach him and ask him to rid your mind of it. There are certain things you want today, for yourself or for other people; now is the time to ask God for them. They may be quite childish and unimportant things; doing well in a game, perhaps, or getting away with it when you haven't prepared your work properly—it doesn't matter, offer those needs in petition to God. You've done something you're ashamed of; offer him your penitence. You have quarrelled with somebody; put aside your enmity, let it be burnt up in the fire of our Lord's charity. You have made some good resolve; dedicate it, now, to God's service. Your mind turns to the thought of a friend, of your family at home; say a prayer for them, commit them to God. Every thought that flashes across your mind can be irradiated with the fire of our Lord's sacrifice, like the little motes of dust in the air that show up in a sunbeam. Even the distractions you have are so many sticks for the burnt-offering, so much raw material for the miracle that is about to happen.

I don't mean that the Offertory is the most important moment in the Mass. Of course not; what God does in the Mass is very much more important, obviously, than anything man does. But I'm mentioning this because it seems to me the Offertory is the part of the Mass we most neglect; the part of the Mass whose dignity and meaning we most forget. Whence shall we provide bread here in the wilderness? There is a lad here that hath five barley loaves. Whence shall we bring down the Body and Blood of Christ onto our altars? Look, Lord, I have something to offer—this and this and that.

I suppose there is no form of discouragement commoner among moderately good Christians than disappointment over the small effect which frequent reception of holy Communion has in our lives. It ought to make so much difference; it seems to make so little. After all, what is happening in holy Communion? What is happening is that our Lord is transmuting us into himself. In the ordinary way, when we eat something we are incorporating it into ourselves, making it a part of ourselves. But in this heavenly Banquet it is the other way round. By partaking of the Blessed Sacrament we do not incorporate it into ourselves; we incorporate ourselves into it. I live, as St. Paul said long ago, and yet it is not exactly I who am living any longer; it would be more true to say that it is Christ who is living, continuing the work of his Incarnation, in me.

That is what holy Communion means. And then, when we compare that with the actual facts, the observed facts, as far as we are in a position to observe them! We find ourselves going away from church and getting into a bad temper or talking uncharitably within the same half-hour; a day or two later, perhaps, we yield to worse temptations, which we had renounced altogether when we were last at confession; why is it, we ask, that holy Communion hasn't done us more good?

Well, there are all sorts of answers which can be given to that question, all of them containing a great deal of truth: as, that we are not always good judges of our own progress; that the effect of the Sacrament is proportioned to the stage of spiritual development in which the recipient is, and we are only children, only beginners; that it is something if frequent Communion only helps us to mark time, keeping our faults in check—the day's food for the day's march—without, as yet, leading to actual improvement. But the answer which I want to suggest, in case it applies to anybody here, is most simply put in the form of another question—Are you sure that the reason why you get so little out of your Communions isn't that you put so little into them; you don't receive, because you don't give?

How often, as we have already reminded ourselves, we just dream away the first part of the Mass and only awake with a shock as the bell rings at the Sanctus! And then we comfort ourselves by reflecting, Well, after all, the important part of the Mass is still to come. Yes, that's quite true; the amazing part, the miraculous part, is still to come. But, you see, you *have* missed *something*—the time when the priest was offering the unconsecrated bread and wine in the name of the congregation. And that was the time when you should have been offering yourself, and all that you have, your sins, your weaknesses, your needs, your hopes, your comforts, your career, your future, utterly into God's hands. Our Lord, says the *Imitation,* gives his grace where he finds vessels empty to receive it. Do we empty ourselves of self, make a free gift to him with both hands of all we have and are, before he comes to us in holy Communion? Or are we, half-consciously, making reserves with him all the time,

"Dear Lord, I am ready to give up everything for you, except perhaps this. . . . Dear Lord, I want you to make me very holy, but not quite as holy as all that", and so on? What would have happened to the story of the Five Thousand if the boy had said to St. Andrew, "I'm sorry, but I'm afraid I want them"?

You see what going to Mass should be. It's quite true that while you are at school you go to Mass whether you want to or not; and we all of us have a slight prejudice against being told to do things whether we like it or not. We don't want to be like the child on the sands at Margate —his mother stood over him beating him about the head and saying, "Now, Albert, you've come out here to enjoy yourself, and enjoy yourself you shall." But then, that's the whole bother about being at school, that everything has to be done by numbers, because that's the only way of getting it done at all.

It would be very nice if Masses were going on all the morning, and you could get up in the middle of class whenever you felt like it and say, "Excuse me, Sir, I'm going to Mass now." But your convenience has to be regulated by the convenience of other people, in this as in everything else. You go and have your meals, not when you feel like it, but when other people are going in to meals; you go to bed, not when you feel like it, but when other people are going to bed; in the same way you go to Mass not when you feel like it but when other people are going to Mass. It's absurd to say, when you leave school, "I shall never go to Mass on a week-day again, because at school they forced me to go to Mass." You might just as well say "I shall never have a meal again, because at school they forced me to have meals", or "I shall never go to bed again, because at school they forced me to go to bed".

The teachers, you see, assume that, being an ordinary Christian, and living in a place where there is a church close by and Masses going on every day, you will want to take, every day, the opportunity of worshipping Almighty God. They don't ask whether you want to; they take it for granted. Like the bridegroom when the priest said, "Wilt thou take Jane Ellen here to be thy wedded wife?" and he replied, "That's what I came for." They assume that you want to be given the opportunity of worship at that hour in the morning, instead of being sent into class for a solid hour before breakfast, as I was when I was at school. And if it doesn't do you any good, that is your fault, because you were content to hang about while Mass was going on instead of associating yourself with the action of the Mass. If you didn't get anything out of it, it was because you didn't put anything into it.

When you are actually at school, to be regular about the Sacraments is almost the easiest thing to do. Come back to my earlier question. Do you go to Mass much in the holidays? Of course it's a long way off, for some of you; but even when it isn't? I've always found it a rather depressing feature of Catholic schools, male and female, that when they reassemble after the holidays *everybody* comes to you and says, "I made my last confession at the end of last term." Don't you think, perhaps, if you went to Communion a bit oftener in the holidays *now*, going to Communion would become more *a part of you,* not just a thing one does? It's the Mass that matters. Build your life round the Mass, and it will stand firm.

Will it stand firm? I don't know; there are such a lot of you; on the average, some of you are likely to make a mess of things. God knows it's a pretty beastly sort of world you will be going out into, when you leave school. I wonder what you are going to do? Anyhow, there will be plenty of opportunity to make a mess of things; you will be tempted to take rash decisions, get betrayed into a wrong marriage, or get mixed up in unhallowed causes, half thinking that what you do is right. If anything of that kind happens, please God it won't, try to remember two things, if you forget every other word I've said. One is this; never give up your confidence in our Blessed Lady; she can't let you down. And the other is this; whatever sort of fool you've made of yourself, don't doubt that there is mercy for you even at the last moment, if with your last breath you will tell our Lord you are a sinner, and sorry for your sins.

13 *Holy Communion*

YOU may compare the crucifix to the portrait of an absent friend, by means of which we contrive to keep him in our memory and to let ourselves be influenced by that memory as we would be influenced by his presence. But there is, as we all know, another way in which we can remind ourselves of an absent friend, one which makes less appeal to the senses but more to the imagination; we can keep about us some relic of him—some present he has given us; or some object which he was in the habit of using, which we are accustomed to seeing in his possession. And it sometimes even happens that a lover or a mother will try to awake more intimate memories still, by keeping an actual personal relic, a lock of hair, probably, shut up somewhere in an old drawer, but taken out now and again to be looked at and to be pressed to the lips. It is in the same spirit that we keep in our churches the relics of the saints. As we kneel before these we are in actual contact with something that was once part of themselves, and we hope with good reason —the whole of the Christian tradition encourages us in the hope—that a virtue and an influence still remains in such objects which will be effective in our lives.

God is not really an absent Friend at all; he is close to us all the time. We may think of him if we will as present (although without any limitation of space) in the whole world of nature around us; we may think of him as present in the air we breathe, in the sky above our heads, or in the earth under our feet, and we shall not be deceiving ourselves, we shall only be recognizing something which is true. Or again, perhaps with more profit, we shall think of him as directly present to our own immaterial souls, as communicating to them the life by which they live and every movement which stirs them; the motions of the divine grace are, in literal fact, as near to your soul as the wind which fans your cheek is near to your cheek. All that is true; God is never absent from us, and need never seem absent from us as long as we try to realize that he is present. But at the same time, he is not present to us with the distinctness and definiteness with which we can detect the presence of natural objects; there is not, in common nature, anything at which we can point and say, "Here is God"; still less anything at which we can point and say "This is God." And because he knows how much we all depend on our ordinary ways of thinking, he has not been content with all the ordinary gifts which he bestows on us; he has left, to us Christians, a precious relic of himself. And that Relic, I need hardly explain to you, is his presence in the Blessed Sacrament.

I have called it a Relic; but you will see on a moment's thought that there is a great deal of difference between the Blessed Sacrament and the relics of the saints. Imagine to yourselves—it is a familiar experience—some great church which has a personal relic, say the arm of the patron saint, underneath the high altar. And over the high altar, in the tabernacle, is the sacred Host. As you kneel there, you are kneeling before the body of a saint, and you are also kneeling before the Body of Christ. But the manner of the presence is not the same in either case; there are three great differences. In the first place, the body of the saint is visible as a body; if the relic be exposed, you will see the arm looking like a human arm, wasted, perhaps, but still recognizable; whereas the sacred Host, when it is exposed in the monstrance, does not look like a body or any part of a body. In the second place, the body of the saint is only partially present; even if there is the whole skeleton there, the blood will have flowed away from the limbs, and so on. But in the sacred Host, in each sacred Host, the whole Body of Christ is present, his Body, his Blood, his Soul, his Divinity. And in the third place the saint's relic is a dead thing belonging to a person who is dead; and the connection between the two exists, now, only in your imagination. The soul of the saint lives, but it lives in heaven, separated from the body which you see before you. Whereas the sacred Host is not a dead thing; it is the living Christ himself who is there before you.

How is it possible that all this should happen? It is a miracle and a mystery. But let us try to understand it as far as our human weakness allows. There are, clearly, two things about the doctrine of the Blessed Sacrament which make it difficult to believe; two questions occur to us which demand an answer. I do not mean that they are the only questions we might be inclined to ask; St. Thomas counted up the miracles which were contained in the doctrine of Transubstantiation, and I think he made out that there were nineteen of them. But there are two questions which naturally occur even to the most stupid of us. One is, Can God really turn a thing into something else altogether? And the other is, Can God multiply his own Body's presence, so that it is equally present in each Host in the ciborium, so that it is equally present in all the million Hosts of the world?

The answer to both those questions is that he can; and

that our Lord while he was on earth did two things which shew that he could. He turned one thing into another in the miracle at Cana of Galilee; multiplying bread in the wilderness, so that five loaves were nourishment for five thousand people, he shewed that the "quantity" of things, by which they occupy space, was his to control.

In the miracle at Cana of Galilee he turned water into wine. What do you mean when you say that? What idea does that phrase convey to your mind? Oh, you say, now that you put it like that I am not quite sure what it does mean. . . . Let me see, it would be something like this; there were the water-pots of stone full of water, and while the water was being poured out our Lord miraculously altered it so that it had properties which it had never possessed before. Instead of being colourless, it came out red; instead of being tasteless, it tasted like wine; instead of being a mere harmless liquid of which you could drink as much as you liked, it had the effects of fermented liquor; it had the power to quicken the heart's action and to brace the nerves as wine does. Yes, but was that all? Did he do nothing more than alter the colour and the taste and the medical properties of the water? Because if so, you see, it is nonsense to say that he turned water into wine. What was left in the water-pots after the miracle was not wine, it was water still. It was water which had taken on a new colour, a new taste, new power to intoxicate; but it was water, not wine. And, you see, you have made our Lord guilty of a deception; you mean that he offered to the wedding-guests as wine something which was not really wine. That will not do; that is not what the Bible says. It was not merely the appearances of the thing which our Lord altered; he altered the reality as well. Or, if I may use philosophical terms, it was not merely the accidents that he altered, but the substance.

You thought that he only altered the appearance without altering the reality. I have pointed out that you are wrong, that he altered both the appearances *and* the reality. Now, in the miracle of Transubstantiation, he does not alter the appearances without altering the reality; he does alter the reality without altering the appearances. The consecrated Host has still the appearance of bread; the consecrated chalice has still the appearance of wine. But the underlying reality has changed; in reality, in spite of appearances, it is the Body of Christ which lies on the paten; it is his Blood which is contained in the chalice. Do not say that he has deceived you; he has done the exact opposite. A deception is something that is less real than it looks; but the holy Eucharist is just the opposite; it is something actually more real than it looks.

At Cana of Galilee our Lord shewed that he could turn one thing into another; that he could alter the reality of natural objects. And when he fed the five thousand in the wilderness he shewed that he could alter the quantity of natural objects and their occupation of space.

And if he could do that, while he was on earth, does it really surprise us that he should be able, now he is in heaven, to multiply his own Body and Blood in the holy Eucharist? We have seen that in the miracle of Transubstantiation what is changed is not the accidents of the bread and wine, not the appearances which we can note with our senses, but the substance, the underlying reality. Now quantity, which makes possible extension in space, is an accident, not part of a thing's substance. So that when the words of consecration are pronounced the quantity of that which lies in the ciborium remains unchanged; the Hosts become neither larger nor more numerous than they were; it is their substance that is changed, not the accident of their number or the accident of their size. And consequently when you receive the Host, for all the smallness of its dimensions, you receive not a part of our Lord's Body but all his Body —mathematical considerations of space and extension in space do not enter into the question, because we are talking about the substance, the reality, not the external appearances. Let me give you an obvious illustration—you are holding a looking-glass in your hands, and you can see reflected in it your own features and, behind them, the ceiling of the room in which you are standing. Then, clumsily, you drop the looking-glass, and it falls into pieces on the floor. Now, will each of those pieces reflect part of your face, part of the ceiling? No, each single piece reflects the whole of the ceiling, the whole of your face, as before. So it is if the sacred Host is divided; each division of it is— what? Not part of our Lord's body, but the whole of our Lord's body. It is the substance, not the accident of size, that counts.

I said just now that there is nothing in common nature at which we can point and say, "This is God," or even, "Here is God"; he is not here or there more than anywhere else. But in this supernatural gift, this miraculous Relic which he has left us to remember him by, his presence is brought within the reach of our human thought. We can point to the tabernacle in which the Blessed Sacrament is reserved, and say, "Here is God." We can point to the Host that glistens before our eyes in the monstrance, and say, "This is God." That Divine Presence which is always with us, all around us, is focussed as it were and isolated in this mystery of the holy Eucharist; the whole of the Godhead is confined within a little space, as the whole vast circle of the sun can be reflected in a single puddle.

How he must love us, how he must long for our intimacy, to have done all that for us! In the first place, you see, he became incarnate as Man. The whole fulness of the God-head dwelt in a human form; dwelt for a time in the form of a little baby on his mother's breast. The God who made all things and upholds all things by the word of his power became part of his own creation, as it were, confined himself within the conditions of time and space, for our sakes, so as to bring himself closer to us. But, you see, that wasn't enough for him. If he was to live the life of an ordinary man, that life must come to an end; his presence on earth would be limited to a particular period of human history, and those who were born, like ourselves, long after that period would no longer be able to say to one another, "Jesus of Nazareth passes by." And again, a human body like any other natural object is present at one single point in space, and is absent from all other points in space; if our Lord were living now, as Man, in Palestine, only those of us who are rich enough to afford the journey to Palestine would be able to go and see him. So he determined at once to perpetuate and to universalize the miracle of his In-carnation by the miracle of the holy Eucharist. It had got to be possible for us, living nineteen centuries after the time of the Emperor Tiberius, living far away from Pales-tine, at the other end of the next continent, to say, "Here is Christ! Here is the human Body of Jesus of Nazareth present in our midst!" That is what the Blessed Sacrament makes possible.

But even that was not enough. Just think for a moment what it would be like—it is an impossible supposition, of course, but just think what it would be like—if we Chris-tian people had all the other opportunities of worship to which we are accustomed, the Mass, and the Blessed Sacra-ment in the tabernacle, and Benediction, and processions of the Blessed Sacrament, but there were no such thing as receiving holy Communion. We should, to be sure, admire the wisdom of God's Providence towards us; we should be infinitely grateful to him for bringing himself so close to us; we should still be able to sing, with loving admiration:

> "Oh see, within a creature's hand
> The vast Creator deigns to be,
> Reposing infant-like, as though
> On Joseph's arm or Mary's knee."

We should still be able to say, with a prouder boast than the Jews had of old, "See how close our God comes to us." But he wanted us to be able to say something better than "See how close our God comes to us." He wanted us to be able to say, "See how close my God comes to me."

Personal religion, not a relation between our God and us, but a relation, an intimacy, between my God and me. That is the secret. And so he does not leave us to come to him, and kneel at a little distance and adore him, at Mass or Benediction. He comes to us in holy Communion, comes close to us, gives himself to us, incorporates us with himself, makes himself part of us in order that we may make ourselves part of him; the Divine Lover will be content with nothing less than that. You remember the centurion who came to our Lord, and asked him to heal his servant, who was ill? The centurion was a man accustomed to military discipline, to having his orders carried out; "I say to this man go, and he goeth, and to another come, and he cometh, and to my servant do this, and he doeth it"—he was accustomed to have people running errands for him, and if he gave an order, he assumed that it was carried out, he did not bother to go round himself and see whether it had been carried out or not. And he expected that our Lord would have the same feelings about his miracles; he was so busy, so crowded with petitioners, that there was obviously no time for him to go round himself attending to the needs of each one in turn. It was enough that he should speak the word, and some ministering angel would hasten to the sick man's bed-side, and the illness would disappear. "Lord, I am not worthy that thou shouldst come under my roof, but speak the word only, and my servant shall be healed." And our Lord consented to do as he was asked; while he was living on earth as man, he was confined to one point in space and to one exercise of activity at a time—he could not be everywhere at once, attending to everybody at once. But now that he lives glorified in heaven it is not so. We still say, or rather the priest says in our name, as we kneel at the altar rails, "Lord, I am not worthy that thou shouldst come under my roof, but speak the word only, and my soul shall be healed." But he will not have that; he will not be content with that, now. He will put himself personally at our disposal; he will come to each one of us severally, and will banish by his own presence the evils that afflict our souls.

Jesus Christ is the same yesterday, today, and for ever. He waits for you in the ciborium, your Friend of yesterday; the Friend whose intimacy you have so often forgotten, so often half despised, more than once have even betrayed. All that he has forgiven you, as a friend does; true friendship, unselfish friendship, will feed upon such forgiveness, rejoices to support with its own strength another's weakness. You have proved yourself unworthy of such a Friend; yes, but if you have acknowledged yourself unworthy, then your very unworthiness draws him to you the more; "so frail, so erring," he says, "is this my human creature; shall I not open my Heart to it the more, because it needs me so much?" Your Friend yesterday; all the faults of all your yesterdays are as if they have never been. Your Friend today, today, when you are so little conscious of the need for such friendship.

Today you are young, and live from day to day, accepting as a matter of course all the gifts God showers upon you, and this supernatural gift among the rest. The urgency of living, of fending for yourself and making decisions for yourself, has not yet come upon you; earthly loves have not yet enthralled you and then played you false; you have not experienced, yet, the loneliness which demands, and drives you back upon, a supernatural friendship. And yet his Love, so little felt and so little realized, is strengthening itself, please God, in your heart, waiting for the day when you will need it more. Your Friend today, invisibly supplying you from day to day with the strength you need, and do not know that you need it.

Your Friend for ever—the whole setting of your life, the whole grouping of your human relationships, will be changed, probably, twenty years from now. Death and distance and the claim of rival interests will have broken up those intimacies which now seem to you so enduring and so inevitable; your school, by that time, as likely as not, will only be a memory to you, a place of ghosts when you revisit it. But his friendship will remain unaltered; his Presence in the Blessed Sacrament, perpetually renewed by the miracle of consecration, will still wait for you, the same as ever. And at last, with death, the final severance must come, and all earthly ties, even the dearest, must slip away from you; even then, this friendship will be yours, and he will come to you, still unchanged, in your Viaticum, to strengthen you for the last passage of all. Your Friend for ever—he waits for you there, in the Host that is to be yours tomorrow, incarnate for you, crucified for you, risen for you, hidden under these sacramental veils, as if there were no other creature that had a claim upon his bounty, for no other end than to be united, once again, with you.

14 *The Rosary*

MANY of you have in your pockets, at this moment, a collection of little beads strung together on a wire, your rosary; probably some of you are engaged at this very moment in trying to untie the knots in it. It's extraordinary how knots do form themselves in one's rosary, isn't it? As if the devil were continually at work trying to prevent you from having the opportunity of saying it. And extraordinary, too, how difficult it is to take the knots out of it when it's in your pocket; as if your guardian angel were determined that you shouldn't do two things at once. Let's talk about what the Holy Rosary means and why we are constantly encouraged to say it.

The Rosary isn't a string of beads. In saying it, we use a string of beads, but the Rosary itself isn't a string of beads; it's a series of meditations. The beads are only there, if you come to think of it, to help us count. Of course, I expect most of you have learned to count by now, under the able guidance of your mathematical masters; but all the same it's convenient to have a tally to count with, and make sure you are not counting wrong. When the emperor Darius invaded Scythia, about three hundred years before Christ, he built a bridge of boats over the river, and left part of his army to look after it while he was away campaigning on the further side. And when he did so he tied sixty knots in a rope, and said to the people who were left behind: "I mean to be back before sixty days are over. So will you please untie one knot each day, and if you find yourselves untying the last knot, you needn't wait any longer, you can just go home, because it will mean that I have been defeated by the Scythians and shall never come back at all." He didn't want, you see, to have his men arguing with one another and saying: "Now was it a Monday, or was it a Wednesday, when the boss told us to start counting?" They were to undo a knot every day, and it was sure to be all right.

And the reason for having knots, or rather beads, in a rosary is so that we can slip them between our fingers and count without noticing that we are counting. Because it's extraordinary how even the most mathematical of us can't count unless we devote our attention to it. A schoolmaster I knew, when he was walking in the street and met a boring person who started saying what a fine day it was and all that sort of thing, used to reply, "Don't talk to me; I'm counting," and so passed on. You must have noticed before now how one always has to start counting again if one's interrupted in the middle. And when we say the Holy Rosary we let the beads do the counting for us, so that we can be otherwise engaged.

Otherwise engaged; yes, but exactly how? What is it that we are supposed to be doing while the beads slip through our fingers? "Oh," you say, "that's easy enough. I'm saying Hail Mary's." Yes, you're saying them; but are you thinking them? If you can lay your hand on your heart, and tell me that all through those five Our Fathers and fifty Hail Mary's you are *thinking,* all the time, about what you are saying, that you are really lifting up your heart to God and to Our Lady, then I've no criticism to offer, except that I think you are an extremely lucky person to be able to do it; by all means go on doing it. But you know, with most of us, saying the same form of words over and over like that does tend to make us rather inattentive. We find ourselves thinking about whether it is going to be a fine day tomorrow and a whole lot of things like that. And if our attention was going to wander all the time anyhow, what was the use of having those beads to do the counting for us? We might just as well have been concentrating our attention on that. I daresay you know the unkind remark somebody made about knitting. Knitting, he said, was invented so that women should have something to think about while they talked. Well then, why shouldn't we simply count our Hail Mary's so as to give us something to think about while we pray?

No, it's all a bit more complicated than that. The holy Rosary is meant to be a meditation, or rather a series of short meditations. And in a sense we are not meant to think about the Hail Mary's while we say them; we are meant to be thinking about something else. Don't let me give you scruples about this; if it's a matter of getting an indulgence, you get it by just *saying* the Rosary, whether you meditate or not. And it is a very good thing to do to *say* the Rosary, even in circumstances which make it almost impossible for you to meditate; as for instance when you have got a tooth-ache, or when you can't go to sleep at night. But the ideal way to say the Rosary is not just to repeat the Hail Mary's while you finger the beads. Ideally, the beads ought to be occupying your fingers, to keep you from fidgeting (always hold the beads tight, don't fidget with them, or you will find yourself getting distracted), and the Hail Mary's ought to be occupying your lips, so that you may be certain you are paying at least some kind of external honour to God. But meanwhile your brain ought to be doing something else;

your brain ought to be meditating on the fifteen Mysteries. To help you to do that, I want to go through the fifteen Mysteries now, only dwelling for a very short time on each. We begin with the Joyful Mysteries.

First, the Annunciation. The angel tells our Lady she is to become the Mother of God, and she says, "Let it be according to thy word." What would have happened if she had said, "I'd rather not"? Well, of course God knew beforehand that she wouldn't. But you do see, don't you, that in a sense our Lord's coming and the salvation of the world depended on our Lady saying Yes, when she might have said No? But her will loses itself at once in the will of God, adheres to it, like the needle to the magnet. And of course that adhesion of the will to God is really the whole of prayer; and when you and I have learned to unite ourselves all the time with our Lady in her Annunciation, accepting God's will without hesitation or murmuring and making it our will simply because it is God's will, then we shall have really begun to pray.

Next, the Visitation. When you hear a piece of good news, especially when it's something which increases your sense of self-importance, it's apt to make you a bit self-centred. You don't, for the time being, worry much about other people or their affairs. What does our Lady do, when she hears the good news? Go down on her knees and have an ecstasy all by herself? No, she arose with haste, and went into the mountain country to see her cousin Elizabeth, having just heard that she was going to have a baby. With haste—she doesn't lose time over it; the mountain country —she takes trouble over it; her first thought is to go and be useful to somebody else. So let's ask our Lady, in union with the mystery of her Visitation, to make us more unselfish, make us think more about other people and seize upon

opportunities to do a good turn to other people, instead
of letting our love of God spend itself upon feelings of
devotion and of anxiety over the destiny of our own souls.

And then, the Nativity. Here we have to think about our
Lord and our Lady as well. We have to think about the
great humility which our Lord shewed, in becoming not
merely Man but a little Child for our sakes, with all the
undignified weaknesses of childhood. And that humility of
his communicates itself to, is echoed in, the attitude of his
Blessed Mother. She is content with a stable for her nursery;
she doesn't complain about the inn-keeper turning her out
of doors, she makes the best of the situation, like a practical
woman, and lays her Son in a manger, because it's the best
substitute for a cradle that can be found. Humility, you
know, depends an awful lot on just taking things as you
find them, making the best of things as you find them, not
running round in circles and complaining that the world
is treating you badly. Let's ask our Lady, then, when we
meditate on her Childbearing, to let us share in that
simplicity, that unpretentiousness of hers, always thinking
ourselves lucky for what we get.

And the Presentation—we call that one of the Joyful
Mysteries, but you would have thought it was a sad occasion
for our Lady, to go up and offer her Son to God in the
temple, and be assured in the temple that this offering was
really going to be accepted; that the Child in her arms was
going to be rejected by his people, and that a sword would
pierce her own heart in the process. But you see, it becomes
one of the Joyful Mysteries because our Lady knew how
to take a prophecy of that kind. She kept all these things
and pondered them in her heart; schooled herself beforehand to be ready for the day of suffering when it came. Let's
ask her to inspire us with resignation to God's will, when

it is God's will that we should suffer; leaving it all in God's hands.

And then the Finding of our Lord in the Temple—or rather, the losing and finding of our Lord; our Lady only had the joy of finding him at the expense of all the pain she had in looking for him; her joys were rather sorrowful joys after all. I suppose we ought to ask her, in honour of that mystery and by the grace of that mystery, to be less dependent than we are—how miserably dependent we are!—on earthly consolations. We can't be properly resigned to God's will unless we are prepared to let him take away from us the people we are fondest of; they are in his hands, not ours. And we can't even be properly resigned to his will if we depend upon the feelings of devotion and consolation which we sometimes get in our prayer. That sense of his nearness to us is a thing which comes and goes as he wills; we have no right to expect it when it is given and no right to complain when it is taken away. Let us accept all the joy God gives us in life, as our Lady accepted her joys, always with the reflection that the joys of earth are only fugitive.

When we come on to the Sorrowful Mysteries, you will see that our Lady disappears from the scene; she wasn't even present, for example, in the Garden of Gethsemani. But I don't think there's any doubt, do you, that she shared those sorrows, though it were only from a distance? Our Lord had dropped so many hints of the destiny which was to overtake him, that I don't think there can be much doubt she spent that night of Maundy Thursday in agony, even as he spent it in agony; you know very little about mothers if you doubt that. Let's accept, in union with that unseen, that unwitnessed agony of hers, all the anxieties and the worries that God is going to allow to befall us; uncertainties about our own future, disappointment in our friends, all the strange depressions and discouragements that are rooted in the mind; the weakening of our human spirits, and the fear of death.

The Scourging at the Pillar—we've no reason to think that our Lady saw that either; it was unlikely that she should. But the order for it was publicly given; she knew it was happening, and if she didn't hear the thud of the blows from outside the praetorium, she heard it all too well in her heart. Let's ask her for grace to unite all the bodily sufferings we endure with those our Lord endured for us; let's ask her to wash away with her tears all those sins which we commit by immodesty and self-indulgence, because I suppose it was in atonement for those especially that our Lord willed to undergo so much in his own body. And let's ask her to relieve, with those prayers of hers, all the terrible sum of suffering which there is in this world, especially that which man's cruelty inflicts on his fellow-men, crying in her ears at once for pardon and for pity.

And then there's the Crowning with Thorns; that must have been painful, God knows, but I think what we are especially expected to notice about it is the indignity which all that mockery conveyed. She stood, perhaps, in the crowd outside the praetorium, and heard the roar of mocking laughter which went up when the Jews saw their victim come out dressed up as a stage king—what a good joke! Let's ask her for grace to unite all the indignities, the humiliations, the petty rebuffs and disappointments which hurt our pride with the interior dispositions of God made Man, exposed to public reproach and made to look a fool before a whole city. Those humiliations of ours, how bad we are at bearing them, how feverishly we try to hush them up and to compensate for them, covering ourselves with self-pity, like an animal licking its wounds! But we ought to take them quite calmly, you know, feeling it a kind of honourable distinction to be thought fools, to seem fools, even to *be* fools—why not, as long as it is not our own fault?—in the company of such a Divine Laughing-stock as that.

He called himself a king—dress him up, then, in mockery; he is really the Son of a carpenter, why then, let him turn his hand to carrying wood; so you get the Way of the Cross. Pain there was, and shame there was, in that journey, to pierce the heart of his Mother as she stood huddled away among the crowd, to witness it. But we have spoken of pain and shame already; let's think rather of the intense physical weariness which our Lord must have undergone, after that sleepless night, that agony of mind, those exhausting sufferings of body, carrying two planks, one of them high enough to lift him from the ground. Let's ask our Lady for grace to put up, cheerfully, with all the hard work we shall be called upon to do in our lives, crushing, sometimes, both to body and spirit; eased a little if we indulge in the luxury of complaining about it and getting other people to sympathize with us, but . . . wouldn't the suffering be more like his, more surely united to his, if we could bear it, as he did, without a murmur?

And then the Crucifixion itself, pain and shame and weariness all in one, and with that the agonies of bodily dissolution, experienced by him who was eternal God. Here, we know for certain, our Lady was at his side; and, if anguish of spirit could kill, she must have died there with him. Let's ask him, through her prayers, to accept our lives and our deaths as a sacrifice in union with his own, in reparation for our sins and for all the sins of the world. Let's ask her to make our hearts tender towards other people's misfortunes, treating the tragedies of the world as our own and eager to lighten them as far as that is in our power, instead of shutting ourselves up in our own lives and in our own interests. Let's ask that the spear which wounded him may open our hearts to the love of God and to the love of our fellow-men.

We go on from that to the first of the Glorious Mysteries, the Resurrection;—Easter Day; perhaps our Lady does seem a tiny bit out of the picture here; we associate it more (as the feast of our redemption from sin) with Mary Magdalen, who had needed so much forgiveness, than with our Blessed Lady, who needed none. And yet, although the Gospels don't tell us anything about that encounter, I think our Lord's first meeting with his Blessed Mother after he had risen has a supreme quality about it of freshness, of virginal innocence; the spring morning, with all nature renewed, the human body of our Lord, after all its cruel mishandling, restored to its first beauty, reborn from that inviolable tomb as once it had been born from her inviolable virginity—positive purity, positive innocence. Let's ask her to make us understand that the state of grace to which we are restored when our sins are absolved is not something negative, a mere absence of condemnation, but a real renewal, a re-making, a re-birth; let's offer to her this sudden innocence we have achieved and ask her never to let us lose it again.

The Ascension—our Lord's triumph, for our Lady a second widowhood. Thenceforward, the cenacle is to be her enclosure, her body is still kept a prisoner on earth, while her heart, which could never be torn away from her Son's, even in death, has now followed him into the heavenly places, finds its only home and centre there. When we meditate on the Ascension, let's give him our hearts, to be carried up there like hers; let's want to be, aspire to be, independent of all earthly ties and affections, even the most innocent, even the most natural of them, belonging utterly, by the purity of our intentions, to him.

And the other side of that picture is the coming of the Holy Ghost at Pentecost. Our Lord said that the Holy Spirit would be sent as a Comforter to those he had left behind him; and who was more in need of such comfort than his Blessed Mother, who had lived, all those thirty-three years, only for him? The Holy Spirit overshadowed her at her Annunciation, and she became the Mother of our Lord in his natural body; the Holy Spirit overshadowed her again at Pentecost, and she became, as it were, his Mother afresh, the Mother of that mystical Body of his, which is the Church. Let's unite ourselves with the attitude of holy expectancy in which she waited, during the nine days after the Ascension, for the coming of that divine Guest; let's tell the Holy Spirit that we are waiting for him to come to us, and warm our hearts, and enlighten our minds, and pray our prayer in us, and transform the weakness of our natures, as they are, into the vigorous growth of holiness God wants them to be.

And the next thing we have to think of is the Assumption, our Lady herself taken up into heaven, bodily reunited with him who was the Son of her own body. You know, I expect, the epitaph written on a wife who survived, but did not long survive, her husband: "He first deceased; she, for a little, tried to live without him, liked it not, and died." We don't know for certain how long our Blessed Lady lived on earth after the Ascension; but we can be certain that the time of separation seemed long, and yet that she submitted herself perfectly to the will of God, and only asked to be where he wanted her to be. Let's associate ourselves with that spirit of perfect resignation in which she committed the remainder of her life to God, asking nothing better than to die when it is his will for us, not worrying about whether death comes soon or late, whether it finds us with this or that ambition achieved first or no; let us tell him that, whatever attractions earth seems to have for us, our true happiness lies only in being united with him.

That bodily assumption into heaven was a special privilege granted to our Lady; her Crowning is something which she shares with all the other saints, and indeed with all those Christian souls who will, in the end, reach their heaven. It was the reward of all she did and all she suffered while she lived on earth; so let's unite all our actions and all our sufferings with hers, and offer to her Son whatever merit there is or can be in them, as the saints cast down their crowns before him, glorified in heaven.

That's only one way of meditation on the Rosary; there are lots of others. Don't ever think that saying one's rosary is a thing one is taught to do in the nursery, and can grow out of later on. All the mysteries of our Lord's life and death, all the secrets of Christian perfection, can be found in it, if we will only take the trouble to look.

I5 *Vocation*

THERE used to be a story of a very lazy lodger at a sea-side hotel who generally retired to bed immediately after dinner; but one evening about nine o'clock he came down to the dining-room, and said to the head-waiter, with an enormous yawn, "Excuse me, but could I have a glass of water, please?" So they gave him a glass of water, and he went upstairs with it. A quarter of an hour later he was back in the dining-room, and said, "I'm awfully sorry, but I'm afraid I shall want another glass of water, please." And when he appeared a third time demanding a glass of water (which wasn't a thing he was much in the habit of ordering) the headwaiter said, "Is anything the matter, Sir?" and the lodger with another yawn said, "Well, you see, beastly room's on fire."

Well, rather in the same way as that, I expect some of you have felt it incongruous that we should be devoting our attention to the subjects to which one ordinarily does devote attention during a retreat, as if nothing whatever was going on outside; as if we had forgotten that the whole world is threatened with a conflagration. What's the use, you feel, of talking about the ordinary problems and temptations which belong to everyday life, when this everyday life may be all upset and thrust out of shape, at a moment's notice, by some world-catastrophe? What's the use of talking about death as if it were something that may perhaps be coming along in forty or fifty years' time, when for all we know death may be raining down on us from the air at any moment.

But I don't know whether an atom bomb will fall or not, or what the world would be like afterwards. I'm going to talk on the assumption that the world will manage to straighten itself out without the bomb being hurled, at least for the present, and that you are going to live, most of you, the lives of peaceable citizens. I shall talk as if you would be free to map out your lives according to schedule.

It is curious how often the phrases which we use quite carelessly mean more than we intend them to mean. And there is one phrase in particular which we use in a half-blasphemous way, often enough; and when we use it so, we have the feeling that we are saying something rather emphatic and effective. If we thought over it a little more carefully, we should realize that our statement is a peculiarly obvious truism. And if we thought over it a little more carefully still, we should realize that it is a very profound statement indeed. For instance, supposing that some well-intentioned person, being introduced to you and finding some difficulty in making conversation to you, falls back on the rather stale dodge of asking you, "What are you going to be?" or the roughly equivalent question, "What are you going to do?" It is likely enough that you have been harassed by hearing your parents and your elders talking over your future, and the plans put forward on such occasions have failed to arouse your enthusiasm; and if so you perhaps reply, in accents of suitable boredom, "God knows."

When you say that, you mean to be understood as saying, "God knows, I don't!" You mean that all your own ideas of a suitable future for yourself, such as the idea that you should go out to California and become a movie star, or that you should join the Air Force, or that you should learn art in Paris, have been turned down by unsympathetic people who are responsible for your education; and that they talk, instead, of having you trained to be a chartered accountant, or are negotiating to get you a nice job at the other end of the world. And, finding the division so sharp between your future as you would like it to be and your future as it probably will be, you are inclined, from sheer boredom, to wash your hands of your own career, and assume that probably something will turn up sooner or later, and that something is pretty certain to prove unpleasant. What is the good of asking you about your future, when you are fit for so little and those few qualities you have are so little recognized? What are you going to be? God knows.

And yet, if you reflect for a moment what you are saying when you say that, you will see that you are only stating a very obvious and stale truth. God knows what you are going to be—of course he does. God knows everything, otherwise he would not be God; and your future, although it has not happened yet and is not yet capable of being foreseen by our minds, is nevertheless a fact, a fact still lying ahead of us. God knows all facts, whether they are past, present, or future; that is clear enough. And to say that God knows what your future is does not really contribute to the discussion at all; you might as well say, if somebody asks you what time your train leaves, "Oh, it is in the time-table."

And at the same time it is a mystery, and an awe-inspiring mystery the moment you begin to contemplate it, this knowledge which God has of the future. You see, it is not strictly true to say that God *foresees* what is going to happen to you in later life; he does not *foresee* it, he sees it. And if a human being were to possess complete knowledge of the future, he would still not see it as God sees it. We see events in a series, stretching behind one another in time; God does not see them like that; he sees them all together. He can see you sitting in that accountant's office—or whatever it is—just as clearly as he can see you drawing on the desk here.

God knows what you are going to do; that is certain. And it is possible for you to write those words, GOD KNOWS, as the epitaph of your future, and leave things to take their course; let somebody find a job for you somewhere, or wait till a job turns up for you somewhere, and drift into it, and drift out of it, and drift into something else, and so go on drifting all through your life, reflecting that God knows what will happen to you next, and perhaps deriving a certain amount of comfort from the reflection. After all, it is not only that our future is known to God; it is all in God's hands, and to recognize that is something.

But to return to my earlier phrase, if you could map out your own life, what would you choose to be? As far as I can remember, my earliest ambition was to be a railway guard. I had another programme which involved having a different job for each quarter of the year; during the winter months, I was going to be "the kind of man who smokes a pipe and leans against the wall". Those were, no doubt, unattainable ambitions. But I think it does no harm to ask yourself at this point, not merely "What shall I, in all probability, be?" but as an alternative, "What would I really like to be?" Would you like, for example, to be a cabinet minister? To be a famous artist? To be an enormously rich stockbroker, entertaining shooting-parties in the country? Or just to be a film-star? Or what?

Daydreaming, the spiritual authors warn us, can be a great waste of time. But I'm inviting you just now to spend a minute or two in daydreaming, so that you can be a little clearer about your angle on life. Just try to make up your mind what you would decide to be if there was a Slave of the Lamp about who was prepared to bring it off for you. Just whatever you'd really like best of all. You've got that? Good.

And now, tell me whether that ambition, if it were realized, is calculated to do any good whatever to any member of the human race except you? Oh, of course any kind of successful career is bound to be useful to other people besides yourself; if you went on the films you'd make a large number of people laugh (or wasn't that the kind of star you meant?), and laughing is said to be very good for the digestion. It's not easy to become a successful stockbroker, if it comes to that, without clearing a certain amount of profit for your clients. But what I want to know is, whether that instinctive choice of yours was dictated to you by any notion at all of serving God or of serving humanity, or whether you pitched on that career because it was going to be fun for you? I'm afraid that has caught several of you out. I shan't say anything more about that.

Perhaps you mean to be a priest, if it proves to be God's will for you. I shall talk about Vocation to the Priesthood in the next conference.

Perhaps you mean not to be a priest; that is to say, you have thought of the idea before now, and wondered whether it might not be the life God has in store for you, but have come to the conclusion that it would be a mistake. Don't be in the least shy about saying so; there is never any harm done by having the courage of your convictions. I expect you know the story of the schoolmaster who was talking about moral courage, and said the best example he could think of, to illustrate what was meant by moral courage, would be a dormitory with thirty boys in it, twenty-nine of whom went straight to bed without saying their prayers, while the thirtieth knelt down in front of them all and said his prayers as usual.

And somebody in the class put up his hand and said, "Sir, wouldn't it be just as good an example of moral courage, if you had thirty bishops all in the same dormitory, and twenty-nine of them knelt down and said their prayers, and the thirtieth got into bed without?" There's a great deal to be said for having the courage of your convictions, and refusing to become a priest merely because it's the line of least resistance, and other people seem to think it would be a good idea, and so on. The kind of person who always follows the line of least resistance isn't, after all, the kind of person who is going to make much of his priesthood.

All the same, I am talking now to somebody who *means not to be* a priest, is turning his back on the idea. The chances are, I suppose, about ten to one that you are right in your choice; that your unwillingness, the repugnance which you feel towards the idea, really mean that you have no vocation. On the other hand, there is just the odd chance that you are kicking against the goad; that God is really calling you to the priesthood, and that the repugnance which you feel is just a psychological reaction, a shrinking from taking the plunge. There's no way of telling; I wouldn't undertake to advise you even if you came and saw me about it privately; nothing in the world, I believe, is so difficult as disentangling the signs of a vocation. But if it is so, if God is really calling you, the choice will come back to you later on; perhaps when you've spent five years in the Army, or something of that sort. Don't, then, because for the present it seems clear that is not the way God means you to take, slack off and become a C 3 layman, merely by way of convincing yourself that the thing wouldn't have worked. Go on saying your prayers regularly, frequenting the sacraments faithfully; prove to yourself that, if you abandoned the idea of serving God in the priesthood, it was not through any want of love for him and for his Church.

I'm talking now to other people who *don't mean to be* priests (which is different, you see, from *meaning not* to be a priest). The idea simply hasn't occurred to them; or, if it has, it set up no kind of echo in their consciences; they didn't feel the smallest attraction towards such a life. The chances here are much greater that God doesn't mean you to be a priest; or if he does he means yours to be a late vocation, and it will bring unmistakable signs with it. To you I will say no more, than that every retreat you make ought to be a sort of challenge to you to make sure that you are not missing your true direction in life; it may just be that this retreat is designed, in God's providence, to be the occasion of directing your thoughts towards the priesthood for the first time. In that case, it is not going to be any exhortations on my part that will make you see the way clear. I'll only make one practical observation; the fact that you are fond of serving on the altar isn't necessarily any sign of a vocation. The fact that you worry about other people, and feel as if you would like to be able to help them in their difficulties, is much more likely to be the sign you want.

Well, if God doesn't mean you to be a priest, he means you to be a layman. And that is not by any means such a negative affair as it sounds. Try to realize this—that if God doesn't mean you to be a priest, he does mean you to be a doctor, say, or a soldier, or to join the Civil Service, or to do some one definite thing. He holds between his hands a vocation which he designs for you; and surely, if it is possible for a person whom God wants to be a priest to miss, through his own fault, his vocation to the priesthood, so it must be possible to miss any other vocation which God has for us.

There must be people in the world who are not doing the jobs God meant them to do, and are therefore being less useful in his service—that is putting it at the lowest—than they might have been. For that reason, I think it would be an excellent thing if we did, sometimes, ask God when we are saying our prayers to shew us what job he means us to do in life—instead of assuming that if we are not going to be priests it is a matter of complete indifference to him what we are. And if you're specially keen on some particular career—say, on being a soldier—then tell him that you only want to do this if it is his will for you; and if it proves that it isn't his will for you—if you're ploughed at the medical, for example—then you are perfectly content to let your own ambitions fade out, and take on whatever job is the job he wants you to do.

If your experience is like that of the undergraduates I have to deal with, you will probably find that the range of choice left to you in the matter of your career is a comparatively narrow one; and indeed it is likely enough in the end that you will have to go out to plant chewing-gum in Tanganyika or something of that kind, simply because there appears to be no other part of the world in which people are prepared to pay for your services. You mustn't, for that reason, regard it as any the less part of God's will for you that you should go just there and do just that, because it seems to be the only resource left to you. On the contrary, we ought to be grateful when God treats us like that, because we are saved all the trouble of making up our minds and are quite sure this was what God meant us to do—he'd have provided us with some rival option if it weren't.

And don't make any mistake about this—to do your job well, whatever it is, is the first claim God has on your life. To do it well, not because you want to attract the attention of your superiors and get a rise, not because it appeals to your vanity, to be able to reflect that you have got this thing taped, not because you are afraid of losing it, but because it is the job God has given you, the job you are doing for him. If you became a monk, and it was part of your job to polish the altar candlesticks, you would find it easy to reflect that you were doing this in God's service, because the religious life throws the idea of service, and of humble service, into relief. Well, if you come to think of it, all that must apply to life in the world every bit as much. If you are adding up figures in a bank, you can add up those figures well, for the greater glory of God. The temptation to get bored with your work and to throw all your energies into hobbies and side-lines is a temptation. "In the sweat of thy brow thou shalt eat bread," God said to Adam, and it applies to his descend-ants. "Whatsoever thy hand shall find to do, do it with all thy might." That is the first point.

To do his job, and do it as well as he can—that is the first duty of the layman, as of the priest. There is another func-tion which the layman may have and the priest hasn't—to marry and continue the human species, to marry and bring up a family in the fear of God and in the light of the religion which he has revealed to us. It would be looking rather a long way ahead if I started giving you the sort of advice one gives to young men about to marry, so I don't intend to dwell upon this. I'll only repeat what I've already been telling you in other connections—don't take the risk of making any big departure in your life without asking the Holy Spirit to guide you in your choice of action. There may be excellent reasons for not consulting your parents, for not consulting your friends. There can be no reason which excuses you from con-sulting Almighty God.

One word more to those of you who are not destined to serve God in the priesthood. Do not ever think that because you have not become a priest you are therefore, from the spiritual point of view, a second-class article; do not ever

6*

suppose, unless indeed you have consciously refused the divine invitation, that he is the less your friend, or wants you to be the less his friend, because he does not choose that you should manifest your friendship in this particular way. The Church needs, needs enormously today, laymen and fathers of families who are really on fire with the love of God— nothing less than that.

A year before the Catholic Emancipation Act was passed in England, a young Cambridge undergraduate, Ambrose Phillips de Lisle, became a Catholic. In April 1828 he lay ill, and his life was nearly despaired of, and the cause of his illness was this—although he knew that he had a weak chest, he insisted on riding over from Cambridge every Sunday morning, fasting, to St. Edmund's College Ware, the nearest place where he could receive Communion. I have done the journey myself on a bicycle, and once through an accident I had to do it fasting, and it is not an easy journey; it is every step of twenty-five miles. And when I compare that with the behaviour of the modern undergraduate, perhaps twenty per cent of them ready to walk down a few streets to make their Communion on Sundays, I sometimes wonder whether Catholics are really the same people we were, really the same stock that we were, a hundred years ago.

If you go through life with a merely external profession of the Catholic religion, your neighbours will think none the worse of you, will not bother you, will not hinder you. But the Catholic who means to have a true personal religion will not find his position so easy. You are born to live in a selfish age; an age when most people have not so much money as they would like to have, and have tastes more luxurious than they ought to have. For most of you it will mean self-sacrifice if you are to live as good Catholics and leave good Catholic families behind you. You will find that there are good causes crying for support, good works crying to be done; that there are still misrepresentations of our holy religion current which it is your duty to correct among your friends, not so much by the reasons you can bring forward as by the example of a devout Catholic life. There are only two things, I believe, which are still wanted for the conversion of our country—more love of God among the Catholic clergy and more love of God among the Catholic laity. There will be no lack of opportunity for self-sacrifice in either state; what you need is the spirit of self-sacrifice which can only come to you from the intimate friendship of our Blessed Lord.

16 *Vocation to the Priesthood*

GOD knows what you are going to do. But is the thing which God foresees that you are going to do the thing which God wants you to do? Alas, not necessarily. It is God's will, yes, I grant you that, in the sense that he allows it to happen; if he did not allow it to happen, it wouldn't. But is the thing that each man does the thing that God really meant him to do, really wanted him to do? You can see for yourself that it is not.

Our Lord chose twelve apostles, and one of those, Judas Iscariot, turned out a traitor and a suicide. Our Lord knew, all the time, how it was going to end; all the time that Judas was stealing money from the petty-cash account, our Lord knew about it, and knew more than that, knew all about what it was going to lead to—the thirty pieces of silver, and the rope's end—and yet he chose Judas. He did not choose Judas *to be* a traitor; he had a vocation for him to be a saintly apostle, if he would; to carry his name before the Gentiles, to confess him before kings and rulers, to win the crown of martyrdom, if he would. There is, for each of us, a plan marked out in God's mind, so to speak, of our life as it actually will be lived; but side by side with it a plan is marked out of that same life as God wants it to be lived; and how far those two plans correspond depends on the care we take to find out what God's will is for us and the faithfulness with which we do his will when he makes it plain to us.

Of course, when I say that, you will immediately assume that I am going to talk about a vocation to the priesthood. You are perfectly right; I am. Not, indeed, that I regard myself, or would have you regard me, as a particularly competent authority in such matters, as a particularly skilled discerner of spirits. I remember a boy coming to me who had quite made up his mind to become a priest, but was not quite certain whether he ought to be a Benedictine or a secular priest. I told him that he ought to be a Benedictine, and I thought that was rather nice of me, because we secular priests have our pride too. Well, he went into the novitiate and stuck that for two days; and then he went straight off to a diocesan seminary and has been perfectly happy there ever since; I suppose he will be getting the subdiaconate this summer. That is just to shew you that I am not really an authority on the subject of vocations. Anybody else could tell you far more about it than I can. But I do just want to put one or two quite commonplace points of view before you.

In the first place, whatever else you make of it, I hope you will agree with me that the question "Ought I to be a priest?" is one that must stand all by itself. It must not be one of a series of questions under the general title "What to Do with Our Sons". I have seen such a series running, not very long ago, in one of the more fatuous monthly magazines, and I am sorry to say that a bishop of another church contributed Number Three of the series, and his article was headed something like "Holy Orders as a Career"; nor was the body of the article much less painful than the title of it.

The question "Ought I to be a priest?" admits of only one alternative; the question in its full form runs: "Am I to be a priest or a layman?" You cannot lump it with the rest and ask: "Am I to be a tinker, tailor, soldier, sailor, rich man, poor man, beggarman, thief or a priest?" Whatever be the right way of looking at it, that is certainly the wrong way of looking at it. If for no other reason, for this—that the career of a priest does not call for any particular set of natural gifts which mark a man out as suitable for it. The natural gifts which can be employed in it are very various; but it does not demand any specialized capacities. You do not need to be a heaven-sent classical scholar, for example, or a heaven-sent mathematician; you need enough Latin to say your office, and enough mathematics to count the collection; not necessarily more. It is impossible, therefore, for a person of ordinary intelligence to say, "I cannot be a priest; I have not got the natural gifts which such a career demands."

And the same principle works in the opposite direction; you cannot say, on the ground of any natural gifts, "So and so is just the kind of person who ought to be a priest." There is no *kind* of person who ought to be a priest; no one kind more than another.

Well, when we have got that much clear, we try to solve the question from the other end. We think to ourselves that perhaps the only people who are meant to be priests are the people who are very much holier and much more self-sacrificing and devout than their neighbours; really half way to being saints already. And that seems to be a complete solution of the problem for you; because you feel certain that you are not any better than your neighbours in ways like these. And if you read spiritual books that are meant for priests, like Bishop Hedley's *Retreat,* you will probably get that same sort of impression, that all priests live on a plane of spirituality which would be quite impossible for an ordinary person like you.

And then perhaps you think of some priests you know,

and the retreat fathers you have seen, and you say to your-self, "Well, dash it all! . . ." I cannot remember which school it was the story came from about the boy who was asked to give a list of the corporal works of mercy; and he said the first was to give food to the hungry, and the second was to give drink to the clergy. That shews, doesn't it, a quite dif-ferent estimate of the clerical vocation. So that this test does not do either; priests, we hope, are all *aiming* at their own sanctification; but they do so from very different levels; they do not start, at any rate, by being half saints already, and if the bishops did not accept anybody for ordination unless he was half a saint already, you and I would have a precious long distance to go on Sunday if we wanted to hear Mass.

And so we get driven back on the bare doctrine of voca-tion; the doctrine, I mean, that God does want some people to serve him as priests, and wants other people to serve him as laymen. Neither extraordinary natural gifts nor extraordi-nary supernatural gifts will mark the difference. And it is not always his best friends that he calls to serve him in the priesthood; St. Thomas More, for example, tried his voca-tion as a Carthusian and found he had no vocation; yet he was saintly, I think, in his life as well as in his death. The question, therefore, becomes a personal one for you. You have not to ask, Does God want *all* his friends to become priests?—you have to ask, Does God want this particular friend of his, me, to become a priest?

Now, I think this is a perfectly fair thing to expect, though it is ordinarily a presumptuous thing to expect this or that of God. I think it is fair to expect that, provided you do your best to cultivate his friendship and to be worthy of his friend-ship, God will let you know if he does want you to become a priest. He will give you some indication of it, some drawing towards himself. When I say that, you must not expect too much; you must not expect a kind of supernatural revelation, visions or ecstasies or anything of that sort. No, but the idea will come to take shape in your mind, at first perhaps only as a vague and distant possibility, then more clearly as time goes on; your friendship for God will make you want to do something for him, and your desire to do something for him will take this form.

Such inspirations come easily, where true friendship subsists. The idea may come simply from within or it may come by some warning from outside which is apparently accidental; from some alteration of circumstances in your life, or from something you have read in a book, or from something you have heard in a sermon—it may even come to you from what I am saying now; God is not particular always about the instruments which he uses, and he sent a warning to the prophet Balaam, you will remember, from the mouth of a donkey.

If you do find yourself wanting, with God's will, to be a priest, commit your aspiration to God with full confidence. If he means you to be a priest, you will be one; there is no need at present to worry about family difficulties or things of that sort. Go on quietly asking him to make you less unworthy than you are of such a vocation. At the same time, remember that the choice in the last resort is not yours; "It is not you that have chosen me, it is I that have chosen you," our Lord says to his apostles. No harm, then, in having a second string in your bow; in thinking out beforehand, if you are already old enough for plan-making, what you are going to do if it proves that God doesn't mean you to be a priest.

I say that because I think there is sometimes a certain temptation for people who are aspiring to the priesthood to go rather easy over their school work, on the ground that after all you don't need much education in order to be a priest. That is not, perhaps, a great compliment to the priests you have met; but I daresay we deserve it. Only, as I say, it isn't certain that you are destined to be a priest; and it is a pity, when you make that discovery, to find that you have really no sort of aptitude for any other job in life. Don't neglect mathematics or chemistry or whatever it may be that you happen to be good at, on the ground that it can't ever help you towards achieving your main ambition in life. Any kind of knowledge can be useful to a priest; and really educated tastes can make him, I won't say a better priest, but a more useful priest; in fact, some people think it is a pity that we haven't more of that kind. God bless you and grant you your heart's desire.

17 *Death (1)*

WHEN I was talking about sin, I kept on saying what a
dreary subject it was. And I suppose I ought to follow that
up by saying that now I am going to talk to you about a
really cheerful subject, a subject that will make us want to
roar with laughter and slap one another on the back; a subject which will make us go away from this meditation feeling
light at heart and care-free and wanting to dance with the
very music of our thoughts. That subject, of course, is death.

What, you don't feel like that about it?

Surely that is very odd. Death means getting away from a
world of shams and appearances, as the epitaph on Cardinal
Newman's tomb says, into the truth; *ex umbris et imaginibus
in veritatem*. Death means not being able to sin any longer;
not having to hold ourselves in any longer and watch our
step for fear we should do the wrong thing or say the wrong
thing. It's like taking the lead off the dog; see how a dog
yaps and scampers all over the place when the lead is taken
off and it can frisk about as it likes.

Death means coming to closer quarters with God, seeing
him, knowing him, loving him as he ought to be loved;
whereas here we are always complaining that we don't love
him as much as we ought to and wishing that we could love
him more. Death means being added to the company of the
saints, seeing our blessed Lady and all our patron saints and

telling them at last how grateful we are for all the care they have bestowed on us and all the good they have done us. Death means being free from all the encumbrance of the body, from its diseases and discomforts, its continual need to be looked after and provided for, and the temptations to excess and indulgence which that brings with it. Death means going home for the holidays; surely there ought to be, about the very sound of the word, something to inspire and uplift us. Death, what a cheerful subject it is.

You don't feel like that about it? Well, let me tell you in the strictest confidence, nor do I.

And let's remind ourselves at once that we have good solid philosophical ground for not liking the idea of death. Your soul isn't something imprisoned inside your body, like the champagne in a champagne bottle, only waiting for the cork to be drawn so that it can froth over and be free. No, your body and your soul are made for one another, belong to one another, are united by a union far closer than any other union of which we have experience in this life. The soul after death, we must suppose, wants its body; it's only the severed half of something which ought to be a complete whole.

It doesn't just want *a* body; it couldn't be satisfied with somebody else's body, as you might be satisfied with somebody else's umbrella when you are going out in the rain. There's a silly story of a man after some public dinner, who was found by a waiter wandering along one of the tables and lifting up the cloth at intervals to look underneath it. So the waiter naturally said, "Lost something, Sir?" And the man said, "Yes, I've lost my meringue." And the waiter said, "That's all right, Sir; there's a whole plateful of them on the sideboard here; I expect they've swept away the one you dropped, I shouldn't look for that." And the man said, "It's got my false teeth in it." Well, obviously it must be something very much worse than losing one's false teeth, to lose your whole body which is made for you and belongs to you and is a part of you.

If it hadn't been for the Fall, this divorce between soul and body would never have happened. As it is, from the moment of your death until the General Judgment, your soul has got to be a disembodied spirit; and it's not natural to it to be a disembodied spirit, and therefore it doesn't like the prospect. So you see there is nothing unphilosophical about minding the idea of death. Let's talk about it quietly.

The other day something happened to me which I hope will happen to all of you sooner or later—sooner to some of you, later to others. I celebrated my forty-first birthday. It is, as you are possibly aware, a common thing among young men at universities to celebrate their twenty-first birthdays. On those occasions, it is customary for the person who has attained his majority to call his friends together and provide them with a certain amount of refreshment, partly solid refreshment, partly liquid, to do honour to the event. And they do so to the accompaniment of a good deal of noise which is often trying to the nerves of the older inhabitants such as myself. Another human being has attained his majority; has become a legal personage and assumed the responsibility for his debts; "I've got the key of the door, never been twenty-one before", that sort of thing; and it seems fitting to the young to attest the fact with a good deal of noise.

Well, I was in a very different case; being forty-one is altogether a different thing from being twenty-one. I had just got past the ordinary turning-point of a human life, supposing that life to be lived to its furthest reasonable limit. And it looked as if the occasion ought to be celebrated in some more serious way.

As it happened, I had nobody dining with me. As it happened, it was necessary for me to dine away from home. So I dined all by myself at a club of which I became a member when I was an undergraduate, and to which I still belong. I dined there, at a solitary table, and thought about the speedy decline of my years and the waste of my youth—so much attempted, so little done, so many opportunities missed; you do not know the sort of feeling, but you will, most of you, by the time you are forty-one. And all around me were undergraduates sitting at the other tables, total strangers to me, yet curiously like the undergraduates who used to haunt the place twenty years before, when I was twenty-one. A little more casual, perhaps, in their manner of dressing, a little softer in the collar and a little looser in the trousers, yet take it for all in all very much what they used to be. The same, only different; living replicas of the men I used to know, so many of them dead by now, killed in war. And altogether it was a very proper setting to make me remember that the world was moving on, and I was moving on, and we are all no better than straws, we human beings, floating on the great stream of time.

It is not difficult to feel like that sometimes; indeed, it is difficult not to feel like that sometimes, if you live as a member of an undying institution such as a school or a monastery is. You hear that old Father So-and-so is just dead, and prayers are being asked for him; and if you have an ounce of imagination it occurs to you to reflect that old Father So-and-so was once a boy in the school like yourself; that, for all the changes and the extensions you have had here, old Father So-and-so used to sit, likely enough, on some bench where you are accustomed to sit now; played the same games in the same fields, broke the same rules, climbed the same trees, in a word, was just the same sort of person as you are yourself, fifty or sixty years ago. And if your mind is one that works forward as well as backwards, you will be led on to reflect that in fifty or sixty years' time you may be an old man like old Father So-and-so, hobbling about and mumbling and telling everybody how much better the school used to be in your time; and then there will be a day when a notice will be posted up in the corridor, and prayers will be asked for the soul of So-and-so, your own name, who used to be in the school as long ago as—this present year! You will realize, in fact, that the life of a school goes on, while the life of its various members comes to an end; it is all like a river, composed of an endless succession of drops of water, and you are just one of the drops, glancing now in the sunlight but destined, sooner or later, to be merged and lost in the sea.

And of course, this whole world of our experience, if you will look at it for a moment with heathen eyes, is nothing else than one long record of Death triumphing over Life. In the spring we go out and see the buds beginning to shoot on the trees and hedges; and, so responsive are we to our natural surroundings, we feel our spirit lightened by the influence; the spring makes us want to try a fresh start in life. We all become optimists for the moment, because the spring is in our blood. Even more elderly people, on whom the effect of having the spring in their blood is usually some form of liver attack, catch in a way the spirit of the season and rub their hands a little over the softer airs of spring.

And yet all that, if you come to think it over calmly for a moment, is just an illusion. Six more months, and the leaves that now shine in their fresh coat of green will be turning yellow and hanging listlessly from the trees, the hedges will be looking dusty and depressed, the flowers will be ready for the bonfire. Life, in Nature, only comes into existence in order to be swallowed up by death. The trees themselves, that burst out into fresh leaf year after year, are growing older, and must topple down some day; other trees will come in place of them, but not those trees; the type remains constant, but every individual thing in nature is the prey of dissolution. Why, the world itself, so they tell us, has a limit fixed to its durability; soon or later the sun's heat will cool, and there will be no more life on our planet. Nothing really lasts, nothing really defies death; there is only a perpetual rebirth in nature, which is the preface to a re-death.

And, if we still look at the world of our experience from a merely pagan point of view, shall we not say the same about the life and death of Man? Pick up *The Times* newspaper any morning, and look at the front page, I mean the outside page—that is where the real news comes. You may be more interested in the sporting page, or in the political news, or in the law reports, but after all what does it really amount to? It will be all the same fifty years hence. The real news of the morning is something like this:

ATTLEBURY. On such and such a date, at such and such an address, to MARY, wife of JOHN ATTLEBURY, a son.

And then, casting your eye a little lower down, you will read:

APPLETHWAITE. On such and such a date, at such and such an address, John Applethwaite, in his ninety-first year. No flowers, by request.

That is the real history of the human race; young Attlebury coming into the world just as old Mr. Applethwaite leaves it. People being born to replace people who have died, much as you would order a new tea-cup to replace a tea-cup that is broken. The food that old Applethwaite no longer needs being consumed by young Attlebury; the air which Applethwaite cannot breathe being breathed by Attlebury instead—a perpetual, meaningless succession of human lives, the new ones not much of an improvement on the old; so we go on, until the sun's heat cools down and there is an end of us.

And notice, meanwhile, from the same pagan point of view, how casual, how arbitrary it all is. Next to old Mr. Applethwaite you will find another obituary of Richard Ashtead, who lived one year and ten months—one year and ten months, while the old gentleman just before him had a run of over ninety! If life is really a good thing, if it is really pleasant to breathe the air and to feel the warmth of the sun, was it really worth while for Richard Ashtead to have just that short taste of it, to go through the miseries of croup and of teething, and never get on any further; never live to shoot a catapult or to hold a bat? Or if, as the pessimists say, life is really a nuisance and a weariness, why could not poor Applethwaite get his release sooner, instead of lingering on to be a burden to himself and a source of endless trouble to his relations? How terrible to think of Death as a blind engine of destruction, striking now here now there without regard to the merit, or the value, or the usefulness, of the lives that are being brought to an end! And yet that is all we shall be able to see in it, from the pagan point of view.

It's interesting to see how the thought of death impressed the minds of people who were born before our Lord came, and therefore had no Christian revelation to guide them. In the early times, before literature began and before people started dramatizing their emotions, they seem to have had two quite different reactions to the idea. One was to pretend —I say to pretend, because after all we can form no idea at this distance of time how far they took it seriously—that death didn't make much difference; that the dead man, when you had tucked him away in the earth, continued to live with some kind of shadowy existence, experiencing very much the same needs, retaining very much the same tastes, as in a previous life. That would account for the way in which they seem to have buried people, in prehistoric times, with something beside them in case they should wake up and feel hungry in the night; or even with a bow and arrows, so that they could go on hunting. When a king of the Scythians died, according to Herodotus, they killed a whole lot of his attendants and shoved them away in the same grave with him, his cook and his personal gentleman's gentleman and all the rest of it. That would be sensible where the cook was concerned, because it would reduce the chances of the reigning sovereign getting poisoned. But to have a whole crowd of them like that looks as if they imagined, in some vague way, that the king went on living and would have need of his servants in the lower world.

But that sort of notion would only last, you see, while men went on living a settled kind of existence, ploughing the same land year after year and being buried in the same graveyards as their ancestors. Once a tribe became uprooted through the invasion of some superior race, and had to go on trek looking for a fresh place to settle in; once it took to living a nomad life, driving its flocks in front of it and never using the same grazing-ground twice, the whole tradition of the family vault would begin to die down. You wouldn't want to bury grandfather in the place where he died, for fear rude strangers should come along and dig him up again. It was under those conditions, presumably, that you took to the rival method of burning instead of burying your dead, and either scattered the ashes about or took them with you in a jar, so that they would always be handy. Such people probably thought of the dead as just ceasing to exist. And it is one of the signs of our modern return to barbarism that we, who live in flats now instead of houses, have seen a revival of the practice of cremation, with an accompanying disbelief in survival after death.

When people started writing books and thinking out the problems of existence, they didn't know what to make of all this business of death. Tradition kept alive the notion of a future world, but as you will see in Homer they pictured it as a rather shadowy, uncomfortable sort of existence. Socrates told his judges that he went to die and they to live, and "which of us goes to a better thing, none knows, save God". The Romans tried to comfort themselves with the reflection that a great many splendid people had died in their time, so it was no great hardship to follow them; and of course, when the Holy Father died, and the voice that could speak to three hundred and fifty millions of believers became silent for ever, it did feel rather silly for second-rate people like you and me to worry about whether we went on existing or not.

But that sort of thing is cold comfort; dying oneself is somehow quite a different thing from hearing about other people dying. And then, of course, both Greeks and Romans tried to persuade themselves that it was a pleasant thing to die in battle, because people went on remembering you and singing songs about you after you were dead. But obstinately the human mind went on objecting that that sort of posthumous publicity wasn't much good, since you weren't there to hear them singing the songs. There was an American, I've been told, who was once reproached in public for having been a coward at the time of the Civil War; and he drew himself up and asked, "Sir, how can you talk like that, when the bones of my substitute are whitening the banks of the Mississippi?"—but that's an unusual case; in the ordinary way, you've got to be either a living dog or a dead lion. The ancients, on the whole, simply accepted the facts instead of facing the problem. The most useful of them was Arria,

wasn't it, the wife of Paetus? When they were both commit-
ting suicide, she got her stroke in first and said, with her very
last breath, "It's all right, Paetus, it doesn't hurt." That is
the sort of thing one really wants to know; but then, she may
simply have been encouraging him, like the person who dives
into the swimming-bath first and swears it isn't cold. You
don't really get much out of the ancients.

Not even out of the Jews?—one naturally asks. No, not
even out of the Jews. There's awfully little in the Old Tes-
tament which suggests a steady belief, before our Lord came,
in personal immortality. As we know, there were people in
his day who expected a resurrection, but it was fifty-fifty,
Pharisees against Sadducees. On the whole, God didn't encourage them much to persevere in his service by promising
to reward them individually in a future world, he promised
to reward their children and their children's children after
they were gone. Our Lord never talked like that; the rewards
he promises lie beyond the grave. And, in order to establish
that currency, to shew that those promises would be
honoured, he must prove to us that we should live on after
we were dead.

For many centuries—how many centuries, the scientist
can only make imperfect guesses—the long duel between life
and death had gone on, and gone on undecided. Always life
refurnished the globe with fresh flowers and trees, fresh living creatures, fresh generations of men and women; always
death swept them away, and life had to begin all over again.
The type was continually preserved—death could not destroy it; the individual continually perished—life could not
give it permanence. And at last there appeared in the world
a Man who set death at defiance. He proclaimed publicly
that unlike other men he had power to lay down his life and
had power to take it up again; he challenged his enemies to

destroy the frail temple of his body; in three days, he said, he would raise it again. His enemies accepted the challenge, and put him to a cruel death. The cross was the crucial experiment; the final stage in the long duel; if this Man could raise himself from the dead after crucifixion, then the empire of death was shaken by a blow from which it could never recover.

You must picture to yourselves a tomb carved out of the rock, with a garden outside it, somewhere near the city wall of Jerusalem. You must picture it standing there in the stillness of a spring day, about nineteen hundred years ago. Lest any human hand should interfere with the dispositions which had been made, a heavy stone had been rolled up to the mouth of the cave in which the tomb was. On the stone a seal had been fixed, so that if the stone were tampered with, the action would nevertheless betray itself. And a few soldiers had been added as a guard, to make sure that everything remained untouched. It is a day of solemn religious observance, the sabbath of the Pasch; there are no wayfarers passing to and fro, for the distance between the city and the tomb is greater than that which the Jewish law allows a man to travel on the sabbath day. The flowers are springing already in the garden, life once more repeating the yearly miracle by which it seeks, vainly, to achieve the victory over death. But inside that cave, inside that tomb, so still in the sunlight, the battle is being fought which is to decide the issue for ever.

Thanks be to God, who giveth us the victory through Jesus Christ. In the darkness of that night, while the soldiers slept at their post, and before the earliest of the faithful watchers were abroad, the stone was rolled away from the sepulchre, and he who had been crucified on Good Friday redeemed his promise, proved the truth of his challenge, by rising from the dead. By raising himself from the dead; that was what made the test so complete, so convincing. He was not content merely to raise others from the dead, as he raised Lazarus, though that by itself would have been enough to proclaim him for what he was, the Lord of life and death. No, he would make the conflict more acute than that; he would himself undergo death, the sentence of our guilty race, would himself breathe out his last breath and be laid in the tomb; it should seem as if at last death had triumphed, had gained dominion over the Creator of the world, and then, effortlessly, without parade and without comment, he would leave his tomb empty and rejoin his friends as if nothing had happened. "That is all death is," he seems to say to his friends; "so completely do I dispose of it, so lightly do I deal with it. I have power to lay down my life, and I have power to take it again."

Since then, for those at least who like ourselves believe in him and in his message, death has no longer been what it was to the men before us, a blind fate that strikes here, spares there, but to all sooner or later brings the end of all joys and of all experience. Oh, it is quite true that we Christians keep up all the old parade of mourning and of funeral ceremonies; we still have hearses with nodding plumes, and stand beside open graves praying into our top-hats, and use black-edged notepaper; that is our official and our human attitude towards the grim passage that awaits us all at the end of life. But, if we really have a personal religion, death is something quite different from all that; it is simply a readjustment of the relations between ourselves and that Divine Friend who, whether in life or in death, is always close to us, and closer in death than in life.

18 Death (2)

THERE was once an old gentleman who enjoyed his meals, and had plenty of money, and was inclined to think the world wasn't such a bad sort of place. The only thing that worried him was that he was getting on in years, and it began to look as if he must be about due to leave it before long. And one night an angel appeared to him in a dream, and said, "If you go down to the bottom of the garden, and poke about in the rubbish heap, you will find a penny whistle there, which is a magic whistle like the ones in the fairy stories. You are allowed to play any tune on it and wish, and your wish will come true. Like the people in the fairy stories, you can only do it three times in your life, so you had better be careful what wishes you choose." Well, the old gentleman lost no time in going down to the bottom of the garden, and there, sure enough, was a penny whistle on the rubbish heap. And he cleaned it on his handkerchief, and although he wasn't very musical, he just knew how to play God save the King on it; and you may be sure he did play God save the King on it, and went back to his study and put it carefully away in a drawer. And the wish that he wished, his first one, was to be immortal. That was a good foundation, he thought; and he would wait and look round a good deal before he wished again.

Well, in one way it wasn't a very exciting sort of wish,

because you can't be certain all at once that a wish like that has come true. But time went on, and the old gentleman didn't seem to get any older, though he got rather deafer, and suffered from one or two infirmities like that. He got ill once or twice, and made the most astounding recoveries, and the doctor told him his heart and his blood pressure and everything was as good as new; he'd never met anything like it. So that was all to the good, but there was another side to the question. All his friends died, and he got tired of going to their funerals. He didn't make any new friends, because he was always telling the same old stories, and talking about the good old times when he was a boy. He got tired of his house, and tired of his meals, and tired of taking off his clothes and putting them on again; and dreadfully tired of the television. In fact, he got tired of everything; nothing seemed to change, and there was nothing to look forward to —just an endless series of tomorrows exactly like today. And in the end he crept upstairs to the drawer in which he kept the penny whistle, and played God save the King on it—he was pretty tired of that too, by this time—and uttered his second wish. And that was that he should be allowed to die after all, but at a moment of his own choosing; nothing was to happen to him until he said the word Go.

And after that, curiously, things went on very much the same as before. After all, there was no great reason to be in a hurry about dying, now he knew that he could die whenever he wanted to. The awful prospect of having to live on and on indefinitely was removed, and he could look round and think about it. After breakfast, he would start on *The Times* cross-word, and he wasn't very good at cross-words, so that occupied him till lunch; you obviously couldn't die with *The Times* cross-word only half solved. And then after lunch he generally slept till tea-time, and it seemed pointless to die when you were going to go to sleep anyhow. And tea, with that false sense of vigour which it produces in all of us, made him wonder why he should want to die at all. The will to die used to come back to him after dinner; but then, it seemed unkind to have all the household woken up and the doctor fetched out in the middle of the night merely because he wanted to die. So he always put it off till next day.

And after that had been going on for some time, he began to admit to himself what the truth was; he was afraid to die. He wanted to be dead, but you can't be dead without dying, and when it came to the actual process of dying he found that he couldn't pull the trigger. I can't stop to tell you all the dodges he tried; how he would drink several cocktails, in the hope of screwing up his courage to the sticking-point, but that only made him feel it was splendid to be alive, and ridiculous to want anything else; how he would read Russian novels in the hope of persuading himself that life wasn't worth living, but always fell asleep in the middle. And at last, feeling rather a worm, but admitting to himself that he hadn't the courage to go through the process of dying by his own choice, he took out the penny whistle for the third time, and played God save the King, and wished that he might die after the common fashion of men, at the hour when death came to take him. But he was, I forgot to tell you, a pious old gentleman, and he made one proviso about his wish; death wasn't to come for him until he had made the nine first Fridays; and when he had made the nine Fridays, death was to come for him as soon as possible, so that he should die in good dispositions, and have nothing to be frightened about on the other side of death.

Well, he started making the nine Fridays, and he found in

a curious way that everything went much better with him now. He had lost the haunting sense of responsibility about the hour of his own death; he began to sympathize more with the troubles of other people; and sometimes when his relations came to see him he would tell them, gravely, that he didn't think he was much longer for this world now; which surprised them, because they had long given up all hope of seeing the inside of his will. And you may be sure he remembered each first Friday as it came, and the sixth Friday came and went, and the seventh Friday, and the eighth Friday; and now he had got into the last lap, and it was wonderful how kind he was to all his relations, and how considerate to the servants, and what a lot he did for the poor, and what a lot of time he spent in church. And then the ninth Friday came, and he woke up early in the morning, rather too soon to dress and go out to Mass; and he lay in bed thinking about the nine Fridays and the revelation at Paray-le-Monial, and wondering whether after all the thing *was* quite certain, since it was only a private revelation and not part of the deposit of faith; and thinking about one or two incidents in his earlier career which had not been very creditable to him, and wondering whether he had made quite clear, in confession, what those incidents were, and whether he had made a good act of contrition afterwards; and thinking about the present dispositions of his soul, and wondering whether purgatory hurt much. And then he looked at his watch, and saw it was time to get up, and stretched out his hand to ring the bell and tell his servant to get the bath ready; and then—well, I'm sorry to say that he decided *not* to ring the bell; he turned over on the other side, and went to sleep again.

And when he woke up—well, when he woke up it's unnecessary to tell you that he realized the whole thing had been a dream, the angel and the penny whistle and God save the King and all the rest of it. If it comes to that, there never was any dream, and there never was any old gentleman; I made it all up, to illustrate the fact that death, or rather the prospect of death, is good for us. And it is good for us for three separate reasons. The first is that it must come some time. The second is that it may come any time. And the third is that when it does come it is infinitely the most important moment in all our lives.

Death must come some time; this world isn't our home, only a kind of hotel where our rooms will be wanted sooner or later for somebody else; life is meant to be only a span of time, and a comparatively short one. When I say it's meant to be, I am, of course, assuming the fact of the Fall. Father Bernard Vaughan, the great Jesuit preacher, was having an argument with some lady who was very strong on woman's rights, in which he wasn't much interested; and I suppose he managed to get her rather ruffled, because she turned on him and said, "Well, anyhow, Father Vaughan, where would you be, but for a woman?" "But for a woman, Madam," he said, "I should be sitting on this hot summer day under one of the trees in Paradise, drinking a lemon squash." If mankind hadn't fallen, no doubt we should be living, and fitted to live, an earthly life which would last much longer and be much pleasanter. As it is, we are living, and fitted to live, on a short lease, and we have got to make the most of our tenancy.

We couldn't, I think, go on enjoying life indefinitely, any more than the old gentleman in my story; we aren't built that way. In the end, we should get fed up with it. After all, some of the suicides you read about seem to indicate that, don't they? Usually, no doubt, there's a reason for every suicide. I always like the story of a house at Eton, where, some years ago, one of the boys tried to commit suicide by taking poison. And the housemaster was very worried over this, because he couldn't understand why it had happened; so, after evening prayers, he talked to the whole house and said what a dreadful thing it was, and if anyone there had any idea why this boy should have wanted to take his own life, would he come and tell the housemaster about it? And they all sat there in a rather strained silence, in the middle of which a very small boy piped up from the back of the room, "Do you think it could have been anything to do with the food, Sir?" Well, I suppose as a rule there is a reason for every suicide; but in some cases it does almost look as if people just got fed up with going on living, and took their own lives for that reason. And I think as one grows older the fear of being dead, or not being able to have any more fun in this world, does become lessened considerably.

Anyhow, whether we cling to life or not, death must come some time; if it were not so, we should be inclined to live too much in the present. We are so short-sighted, you and I, that we are always tempted to put too much of our confidence, to rest too much of our affections, in the transitory, created things which surround us. I'm sure you must have had the experience before now of being asked out to something or other and really rather wanting to go, knowing that it will be rather fun when you get there, and yet—yet at the last moment, when the time comes to start, you begin to hang back and wonder why on earth you accepted that invitation. There is the effort of going there; there is the almost equal effort of leaving off whatever it is you are doing at the moment. Some quite trumpery occupation, no doubt; you are finishing a detective story, or you are cleaning a motor-bicycle, and you feel as if you couldn't possibly tear yourself away. Why on earth was I such a fool, you ask yourself, as to accept that invitation, when I might have been staying quietly at home? In the end you go, simply because you have said you'd go; at least, I hope you are not one of those appalling people who ring up at the last moment and plead an important subsequent engagement. And when you do get there, of course you enjoy yourself thoroughly, as you knew you would. I wonder, isn't that rather the position we are all in about leaving earth for heaven? We know that we shall be happy there; and yet the silly spell which our earthly occupations and ambitions exercise over us is so strong that we should never summon up the energy to take the journey, if it rested with ourselves whether we should take it or not.

God knows our weakness; he knows that our fellow-creatures seem more real to us than the things of heaven, simply because they are nearer to us, and have a more immediate hold over the imagination. So he arranges that the effort of making the last move shan't be left to our choice. Sometimes a very kind host will send his car over to fetch you, because he knows you are not frightfully good at turning up when you've accepted an invitation, anyhow turning up in good time. When that happens, you can't very well get out of it, can you?

That's what death is; it's God's carriage, waiting for you at the door. Suppose you were a prisoner, shut up in a kind of Bastille place, waiting to be executed. Supposing that your imprisonment wasn't a very uncomfortable one; rather boring, because there wasn't a great deal to do, but on the whole you were fairly well provided for. And suppose that every morning the executioner came round for orders, like the cook, and said, "Would it be convenient for you to be executed today, Sir?" How long do you think you would go on saying, "Well, not today, thanks"? You see, there would be always some little odd job waiting to get finished; you would be carving your name on the wall of the prison rather well, and it would be a pity not to get that finished off; or you would have a bet on with one of your fellow-prisoners about the Derby, and it would be just worth while hanging on for a bit to see whether your horse came home; one way and another it would always be, "Well, not today, thanks". We shouldn't really be prepared, if the choice were left to us, to decide exactly when we would like our lives to come to an end. And since that is so, it isn't unreasonable that God should keep the decision in his own hands. That's all death means, to us Christians.

And there's another reason why it is good for us to know, and good for us to remember, that death must come some time. If it were not so, I wonder whether we should ever have the energy to get anything done? Quite often, our reason for doing something quite interesting is that we've got to do it now, because it's probably the last chance we'll get. I expect some of you know the story of the don at Cambridge, who didn't like women going to his lectures, and always took the opportunity to say rude things about them when they did. And one day he was lecturing about the Solomon Islands, where, he said, there was an extraordinary preponderance of males over females in the population; "In fact," he added, "it is estimated that in the Solomon Islands even a woman student of this University would have no great difficulty in finding a husband." Whereupon the few girl students who were in the room looked at one another, shut their note-books with a bang, and started walking out with an air of dignified protest. And the lecturer went on, "I may add, that there is no reason why the ladies should be in any hurry, because the first boat doesn't sail till next Wednesday."

It's that feeling of not having another chance, isn't it, that spurs us on, even the laziest of us, to action. If you went to Oxford for the inside of a day as a sight-seer, you'd go round more of the show places than I've ever been round in all the years I've lived there. You would be determined to make the most of the time at your disposal, like the tourists who try to do their sight-seeing between trains. Whereas I, living there, am in no hurry about it; I can do that, I feel, any time—like the villager who was asked by the motorist, "What's the name of this village?" and replied, "I dunno; I've only been here a fortnight."

Time presses; life is short, and art is long. That's what makes ambitious people start so early, too early some of them, trying to write plays or get into Parliament or whatever it is they want to do. More importantly, if you are anything like a Christian, you can't help saying to yourself from time to time, "Look here, this life is my probation; I shall have no opportunity of doing anything about my soul when it's over. Isn't it really time that I started dealing with that temptation, that I began to adopt reasonable habits of prayer, that I began to try and cultivate a sense of God's presence, learned to love him a little better and conform my will to his, before it's too late?" I dare say you haven't felt much like that yet; but believe me, you will feel like that later on. It's extraordinary how the years begin to slip by, once you're the wrong side of forty.

Death must come some time, and it may come any time. And obviously, if you and I are to be fit to die any moment, we ought to be fit to die at every moment of our lives. It's usual, I believe, for the retreat father to say at this point, "By this time next year one of you will be dead." I'm afraid I don't know enough about the statistics of juvenile mortality to be able to say that with any confidence. But there it is— our Lord was always telling us to be on the watch; to be like servants who don't know when their master is coming home, and therefore don't take the risk of being caught dancing in the drawing-room if he comes unexpectedly. I met a lady once who told me she was on the Riviera, where they were making experiments with the search-light when it was first invented. And she was talking to another lady, a casual hotel acquaintance, on the sea-front one evening, when quite suddenly they found themselves in a great blaze of light. Whereupon this other woman took it for granted that it was the Day of Judgment, and knelt down and told my friend a series of most appalling sins she had committed; which was very awkward when it proved to be only the search-light. Well, we know better than that nowadays. But it remains true that a time will come at which your conscience, all in a moment, will be flood-lit with the glare of the Divine Judgment, and you will be lucky if you don't find, then, that there was more standing against you than you knew. Perhaps we ought to think more about death.

Well, what are we to do about it? Buy a medical dictionary, and mug up all the symptoms, so that every time we get a feverish cold we make certain it's infantile paralysis? I don't think so. Life is a very dangerous business nowadays, and there is plenty of reading in the newspapers to remind us of our last end. There was a man I heard about who was out in China between the two world wars when there was a good deal of fighting going on; he got a cablegram from his mother at home which said "Where are you? Am anxious about you"; he cabled back "Am in Pekin. Am anxious about myself." No, what it really ought to do for us, this thought of death at the back of our minds, is to make us live more in God's presence and go to confession regularly, and take things as they come.

I remember Monsignor Paine, who's dead now but he

used to be Vicar-General of the Nottingham diocese, describing to me the death of his friend Bishop Dunn. I don't suppose there were two more business-like, matter-of-fact men in the whole of the English mission than Bishop Dunn and Monsignor Paine. This was the story, told as far as I can in his own words, of how he went to see the Bishop in hospital when he wasn't supposed to be very ill. "I met the doctor in the passage and he said to me, 'I don't like the look of your bishop.' And I said, 'What, is he going to die?' and he said, 'Yes, he's going to die.' So I went into the Bishop's room and said, 'My Lord, you're going to die.' And he said, 'Oh, am I? Just go out into the passage for five minutes, and then come back and hear my confession.' So I heard his confession, and he said, 'Thank you very much; just turn on the wireless, would you?' He was dead in half an hour." I'm sure that Monsignor Paine himself made just such a good end when his turn came, and I hope you and I may be ready for it as such men are.

Death may come any time. We are frail creatures, and it wouldn't be good for us to know for certain that we had, say, exactly ten more years to live. We should be tempted to put things off; to live carelessly for nine years and reckon on pulling ourselves together in the tenth. How difficult it is to work hard for an examination when we know that it is still more than six months away! Or don't you find that? I bet you do. The sentry who has to keep awake all night guarding some important point is kept up to the mark all the time not simply because he doesn't know when the officer will be going his rounds; he is kept up to the mark *all* the time because he may be inspected *any* time. So it is with us; we are soldiers on duty, and we are or we ought to be proud of it; but we should be afraid of dozing off if we knew for certain when it was that our Captain was coming round to relieve us. We should be afraid that we might be tempted to dally with temptation if we were sure, if we were absolutely sure, that there would be time left to repent in. Death may come any time; in what posture of soul is it going to find us? That is the point.

And here you will perhaps complain that God is not treating us like a Friend; he is treating us more like a schoolmaster; he is, so to speak, putting us on our honour to serve him faithfully, and then coming upon us suddenly to see whether we are serving him faithfully or not; that, you will say, is not the way in which a friend treats his friends. Well, I think that objection is well founded, and I think that if there were only more people in the world who would treat God as a Friend, if it were not such a lamentably common attitude to treat him as a schoolmaster, he might perhaps have arranged differently. I am not just talking at random when I say that; I am basing my judgment on evidence. There is much about the lives of the saints that is of uncertain authority. But there is one assertion which you come across so often in reading the lives of the saints that you can almost pronounce it a general rule—they nearly always seem to have prophesied beforehand the time, sometimes the actual day, of their deaths. Why did God give them this particular grace? Precisely so as to shew that they were his friends, that they served him as his friends, and therefore it was safe to reveal to them, what he keeps secret from us others, the moment at which he would take them out of the world to himself. And this at least is certain, that in proportion as you live on friendly terms with God, death will be relieved for you of half its terrors.

There is still one aspect of death which remains to be considered. Death is the crowning moment of our lives. And that, not merely in the sense that with death comes judgment, and it will be too late to do anything about it. Of course there are such things as death-bed repentances, and I hope there are many; otherwise there will be such a lot of interesting people you won't meet in heaven. Some of you, perhaps, will make a mess of your lives; will be unworthy of the teaching you have had, and sink deep in sin, perhaps in doubt about your religion. But never doubt this, that at your last moment there is pardon for you if you will turn to God and make an act of contrition in the name of our Lord Jesus Christ. Remember that, if you forget every other word I've said to you.

But death ought to be the crown of our lives in another sense; for it is the hour of achievement. When I use that word, I am not using it in the vague and vulgar sense which we, too often, attach to it; when, for example, we pay a tribute to the memory of some great man who has died by telling one another that he "achieved" such and such things.

What people think about us after we are dead makes precious little difference, our reputation soon gets mixed up with somebody else's. Not long ago somebody sent me a schoolboy's answer about John Knox, the great Reformer, who was so unpleasant to Mary Queen of Scots. The answer ran, "John Knox was a cruel Protestant; he wrote a book we have today, the Knox Bible."

No, to us Christians "achievement" means something quite different from the brief praise of our fellow-mortals. When our Lord died on the cross, he said "It is achieved", and we know that he was referring to the sacrifice which he had been offering, all those three hours, all those thirty-three years, to his heavenly Father. And we, so far as we have succeeded in understanding what he wants of us, have offered up our lives as a sacrifice in union with his. We have tried, vaguely and fitfully, to do all that we did for his honour, to suffer all that we suffered for his sake.

And now all that is over, because death has come; and

we wrap it all up in a parcel, as it were, and thrust it towards him, like a bad piece of knitting, for his acceptance. "Take it, Lord; I know I've made a mess of it again and again, this life you gave me to live; the pattern hasn't been your pattern, and there have been loose edges everywhere. But it was *meant* to be like your Son's life, a sacrifice; take it, please, and make what you can of it; I have come to the end of the skein now." That is the Christian's life, the Christian's death.

19 *The Moment of Death*

I HAVE not, myself, a great deal of respect for the people who write books, intended to be scientific books, on what is called anthropology; the people who will describe to you in minute detail what life was like in the ages before history began; what primitive man thought and did, what is the meaning of those stray relics—pictures scratched on the walls of caves, weapons with flint heads, and so on—which primitive man has left behind him. Especially, I think, is it important to take what the anthropologists say with a grain of salt when they start talking about the *religion* of primitive man.

About twenty years ago I remember writing a sort of skit upon this kind of literature, in which I suggested, as a joke, that the celebrations which are still kept alive on the Fifth of November, the bonfire and the fireworks and the effigy of Guy Fawkes, had nothing really to do with anything that happened in the year 1605, or with any historical plot against the Government of England; it was all a relic of some remote religious ceremony, going back far beyond human memory, dealing with the vegetation spirit and the death of the old year and sun-myths generally. All this foolish stuff I wrote twenty years ago as an undergraduate; and then years later I read that some anthropologist, with a great string of letters after his name, had been putting forward this same theory quite seriously, as an explanation of how Guy Fawkes Day came about. So hard is it to parody the anthropologists.

But there are one or two observations which it is possible to make about the religious ideas of the men who went before us long ago, with comparative confidence. We have already noted that men as a rule, even before the time of the Christian revelation, seem to have believed, or to have behaved as if they believed, in some kind of survival after death. And I think you can go further, and say that there were two different forms which this belief took, among different people or in different historical circumstances. You might, as we have seen, think of the dead man's body as enjoying, in the tomb, some kind of continued existence; and therefore you would bury little offerings with him.

But there was, of course, a quite different way of looking at the thing. It was possible to think of the soul as something which was imprisoned in the body during life, and went out of it at death; so that the body of the dead man was of no particular interest to any of his relations. As the poem puts it:

> Sweet friends, what the women lave
> For its last bed in the grave,
> Is a tent that I am quitting,
> Is a garment no more fitting,
> Is a cage from which, at last,
> Like a hawk my soul hath passed.

To people who felt like that it would seem that the soul, now freed from its encumbrances, travelled away to distant and unknown lands, and the body, its outworn garment, was a thing to be thrown away somewhere and forgotten.

And sometimes, instead of burying the dead, these peoples would burn their corpses, because it seemed a handier and more sanitary way of disposing of them. That, as we have already noted, has been happening for some years past among people in our own country who have no strong sense of religion. When they die, they go off to be cremated; and their ashes (if they are kept at all) are carried about in a pot instead of resting, like the bodies of those who went before them, in the companionable earth.

Now observe that those two instincts—the human instinct which thinks of the soul as something closely bound up with the body and the human instinct which thinks of the soul as something easily separable from the body—are both rati- fied by Christian doctrine, and are both corrected by it; to either party we say, You are right and you are wrong. You are right, we say to the burial enthusiasts, in thinking, or rather in feeling, that the body of a dead man is worthy of respect; as something which has been his and will be his again; nay, which has been a part of him and will be a part of him again; you are wrong if you suppose that now it has any life or any human needs of its own. You are right, we say to the cremation enthusiast, in thinking of the soul as something which can have an existence of its own quite apart from the body; you are wrong if you speak of the body as a prison, or a worthless encumbrance—it is something better than that; God would not have given us bodies at all if they served no better purpose than that. For the present, the soul must be content with a disembodied existence, in a state of waiting; but at the final Judgment, when all the tangled clues of our earthly existence will be straightened out for us, the soul will resume its partnership with the body which is connatural to it; and that body with which it will rise again will somehow—we do not know how—be continuous with the body which it belonged to on earth.

That is one difference between the pagan and the Christian attitudes towards eternity—pagan thought gave either too little attention to the body or too much attention to the body; Christian thought steers the middle course between the two. And here is another no less striking; I think it is true to say that, in reflecting on the dead, pagan thought always fears the worst, while Christian thought always hopes for the best. It is true, of course, that the pagan *philosophers* and those who were influenced by them had the notion of a future life in which the good were rewarded and only the wicked were punished. And I think it is true that there were certain mysterious rites into which many heathens were initiated, especially just before the beginning of the Christian era, whose purpose it was to guarantee those who were so initiated the prospect of a life of peace and happiness in the world to come. But the normal pagan attitude about a future life is a depressing one—it is that expressed in Homer's *Odyssey,* where the ghost of Achilles says, "Nay, son of Laertes, speak me no comfortable words of death. I would rather be a hireling, and labour for another man, though he were a man of little substance, than rule over all the dead that are wasted away." This, remember, was a great hero; whose mother, according to the legend, was a goddess, and yet this is all the happiness he finds in the world below. A shadowy, unsatisfactory existence, comparing unfavourably with a life of drudgery spent on earth—that was the best the ordinary heathen dare promise himself beyond the grave.

It is different, isn't it, with us Christians. How naturally we give a dead friend the benefit of the doubt; how naturally we say, "He has gone to his reward" or "God rest his soul."

There *is* a doubt, of course; we know that; we admit that. But it is our instinct to assume, unless we have special reason to think otherwise, that the dead person is happy, whereas it was the pagan instinct to assume that he was being unhappy. Now why is that? What has brought about so significant a difference of attitude as that?

The difference, I think, is simply this; that the pagan thought of happiness in a future world as depending, if it was to be found at all, simply on the merits of the man's life; whereas our hope beyond the grave lies not only in our own merits but in a personal relation to Jesus Christ. The pagan thought of happiness in a future world as depending on our own merits; and how poor a thing those merits are! Even setting aside the theology of grace, how poor a thing human merits are! How many people do you know of whom you could say with confidence that they did more good in the world than harm? What would you say if, at this moment, you had to undergo your Particular Judgment, and were asked to shew cause why you should go to heaven, to point to any one action in your life which shewed anything like a heroic generosity? And yet we hope to go to heaven, you and I. We hope to go to heaven, not as men who have done good service for God's Church, not as men who have left the world better than we found it, but simply as the personal friends of Jesus Christ.

And it is because our hopes of heaven, and indeed of escaping hell, are based on this personal relationship, that I think we ought to be able to consider the subject of our eternity without deserting the principle on which we have been going so far—I mean the principle of insisting on the need for a personal religion. I know that at first sight this does not seem quite natural; we are so accustomed to think of the terrors of hell as a convenient way of arousing hard-

8

ened consciences, to which no higher motive can effectually appeal, that you may quite possibly have supposed I should leave out hell altogether, in talking to you about personal religion. Surely if we are going to be God's personal friends we shall have no need to think about the punishments which he has prepared for impenitent sinners! But that is not altogether the right way of looking at it. It is true that the notion of physical suffering, continued throughout eternity, is enough to stir up the most undevout of Christians, as long as he believes in the Faith. But the further notion which hell involves, that of doing without God for all eternity, is a notion which has comparatively little meaning for the hardened sinner, and has a great deal of meaning for anybody who values God's friendship. The saints, I suppose, at all times have realized the horrors of hell with a vividness and a poignancy of which we ordinary Christians know nothing. It is a part of their spirituality that they should be acutely sensitive of the danger from which God's grace has preserved them—St. Theresa, for example, had a revelation of the place in hell which was prepared for her if she went there. So I am still going to talk to you about personal religion; and I am going to consider what follows death in the light of all that we have been saying hitherto about the friendship of God.

Let us suppose that your death-bed is a peaceful one, and that your faculties remain with you almost to the last. The priest comes, and hears your confession; you mention to him one or two things from your past life, for which you fear that your contrition may have been insufficient. And as you lie dying you still think of your sins; you remember not only the actual offences you have committed, but the occasions on which you have come short of grace, have missed opportunities which were offered you. . . . You see, without any need of going into particulars, how unlike your character is to what it ought to be, to what Christ, your Friend, would have it be. And you think, Yes, but how much more conscious I should be of all this if I were really face to face with Jesus Christ! If I were really conscious of his presence quite close to me, as close to me as my own hands or feet! And, as you think that, a shudder comes over you, and there is a gasp for breath, and then—then you find that hands and feet are no longer close to you, but you are conscious, quite suddenly, of the presence of God, close at your side. That is death.

God is present to you—not more than he was before, all your life; he was there all the time, close to you; but you have only for the first time become conscious of his presence with that full awareness with which we are conscious of outward things. And in becoming conscious of his presence you become, for the first time, fully conscious of your sins and of your sinfulness. Do you know what it feels like to become suddenly conscious that somebody was in the room when you never suspected it, a teacher, say, who has come in when you ought to have been working, and he has stood there and listened to you talking, talking quite out loud, as if he were not there? Surely that kind of shock helps us to understand something about the Particular Judgment. We shall realize suddenly that God was there all the time; we shall be like the sentry in the story who fell asleep on his watch and woke to find the Emperor Napoleon standing there keeping watch in his place.

And, as we realize that God was there all the time, so we shall realize that we have been behaving as if he wasn't there, if that *is* how we have been behaving. We shall realize that though we tried to be his friends, and to prove ourselves his friends, we were all the time neglecting him, hindering his grace, neglecting his inspirations. And we shall not only know that he was there all the time, we shall know how he loves us. We shall be like St. Peter in the Judgment Hall, when our Lord turned and looked at him just when he had made his third denial. One reproachful look, from the eyes of that Friend who has loved us so much, whom we have loved so little in return—that will be our judgment; that will be enough to make us willing to undergo whatever purgatory he has ordained for us—yes, and more than that, if by doing more than that we could make any reparation to the Friend who has so loved us, whom we have loved so little in return. And now, supposing that you saw that Divine Face turned towards you for one moment with a regard of love, and then it was turned away, and you realized that it had been turned away from you for all eternity—tell me, would not that be damnation?

There was a blind man once, they say, who had been blind from his birth, and some kind friends started out to make him understand what colour was like. They thought they would start with scarlet, and they spent a long time explaining to him what scarlet was about. And at last he said: "Yes, I think I've got that—something like the noise a trumpet makes." That was as good as he could do; and not too bad as far as it went. That is the sort of position you and I are in when we try to do what we've got to do next—talk about the world to come. All you've ever been told about saints in crowns playing harps, and serpents crawling about in fiery pits, is about as much like eternity as the noise a trumpet makes is like scarlet. We haven't any apparatus, you see, for getting nearer the truth of the thing. Our imagination is too limited.

And there's another thing which makes it hard for us; we aren't holy enough to see either the glories of heaven or the punishments of hell in their true colours. We are too mixed up with sin to have a clear vision of what holiness means. There's a story, I'm afraid rather an irreverent one, about two business men in Chicago who died about the same time; and they met one another in the life beyond. And one of them came up to the other smiling all over, and said, "Say, heaven's better than Chicago, isn't it?" And the other said, "Yes, but didn't you know? This isn't heaven." It all depends so much where you start from, you see. And we all start from an imperfect world, with fallen natures; and it isn't likely that we should be able to appreciate the flavours, if I may put it that way, of a world in which God's Justice and God's Mercy are made perfectly manifest.

So I don't want to suggest any pictures to your mind; even the pictures which divine revelation gives us, of harps or serpents; because these, too, are only metaphors drawn from human experience; they don't take us beyond human experience. What I shall try to do is to recall to your minds certain feelings we have all had in our everyday life, and ask you to multiply them, multiply them out of all recognition, till they begin to suggest the sort of feelings we shall have, presumably, when we are face to face with the realities of our future life. Our feelings—those, surely, will last with us into a world which it is impossible for us to translate accurately into terms of sight and sound and sense.

20 *The World to Come*

I DON'T think it's the least difficult to see why the fear of hell is good for us, and has an important place in our education as Christians. Because the temptations we have, some of us, to disobey the will of God are so strong, and they wrap themselves up so cunningly in all sorts of disguises, don't they? Sometimes telling us that if we do such and such a thing we shall only be following the law of our own nature, and it can't be wrong to obey the law of one's own nature; sometimes telling us that it is our duty, actually our duty, to disobey God's will out of kindness to other people, to save them disappointment or unhappiness; sometimes whispering that this is a quite unique opportunity of having our own way, and there will be a lot of time to repent of it afterwards. It is very difficult, if you haven't got the fear of hell clearly before your eyes, to remember the unique importance of God's laws, that high dignity which they ought to possess in contrast to all other human values. To remember that what we do really matters—that is difficult, sometimes, unless we can look at the question in the light of eternity, and remind ourselves that an eternity of emptiness and of agony may depend upon our choice.

Yes, if you cannot control your passions in any other way, by all means control them with the reflection that the temporary enjoyment which you covet is not worth the pains of eternal damnation. If you cannot find any better reason for submitting to the will of God, by all means school yourself to submit to it with the thought that rebellion against his will is punished with an eternal humiliation. But, if you succeed in making of your religion nothing more nor less than a personal friendship with God, then the meaning of hell to you will be something rather different. Hell is to have betrayed your best friend and to have lost, for ever, his companionship.

That is good reason why God should threaten to punish our sins in hell. You might be inclined to say, "Yes, it's good reason why he should threaten to; but is it good reason why he should do it? Wouldn't the threat be enough?" But to suggest that Almighty God should play a game of bluff with us, threatening us with eternal punishments which he had no intention of inflicting on us when it came to the point—that would be altogether unworthy of any adequate conception we can form of his nature. He is truth itself, which can neither deceive nor be deceived; he does not threaten what he will not perform.

We have to say, then, that in spite of that love with which God regards every creature he has made, it is possible for a human soul, by misusing his graces, by neglecting his warnings, by defying his will, obstinately, to the last, to bring itself to perdition; to a state in which it no longer responds to the love of God, the love of God no longer acts upon it, any more than a magnet would act upon a piece of wood. By its own fault, it has shut out God's mercies and made for itself a godless universe. While it still lived on earth, the effect of that was not manifest. The sun gave its light and warmth, the earth ministered food, life offered its comforts, to that rebellious soul as much as to any other. And on the other side, that soul felt no need of God; for, in this world in which we walk by faith and not by sight, it is possible to lose sight of God without any sense of deprivation, because we can still huddle creatures closer to us and content ourselves with them instead.

But when death comes, the soul cannot do without God any longer. Creatures vanish from its grasp; it is thrown back on its need for God—and God is not there. It's as if a man who's been playing blind man's buff should take the handkerchief from his eyes and discover that he's gone blind. The godless universe it has made for itself persists; and now, seeing things for the first time in the light of eternity, that soul knows that God is utterly essential to its happiness, knows at the same moment its need for God and that this need must remain for ever unsatisfied. That is the *poena damni,* the punishment of loss, which is experienced in hell. And the theologians talk as if the other part of hell, the *poena sensus,* the punishment of sense, was something quite different, something added on as a kind of after-thought, to make hell worse. I wonder, is that the only thing to see in it? Or doesn't the loss of God bring with it, automatically, a pain of sense?

Do you know what it is to start the day in a thoroughly bad temper, with your nerves on edge, owing perhaps to some foolish mistake you've made, missing a train, for example, or having a quarrel with somebody unreasonably? When we start like that we find, don't we, food for fresh disgust in everything we come across. Each little petty annoyance, hitting your head against something or sitting in a draught or having somebody near you who snuffles or whistles to himself, becomes an intolerable affliction; you want to scream with irritation over the most trifling discomforts. That, you see, is because you are not at peace in yourself; to the man who is not at peace within himself there is no peace in his surroundings either; the world is at war with him.

Now, if you multiply that experience to the scale of eternity, you will see something of what hell must be like. The sufferings of sense are only the echo, as it were, of that utter discomfort which pervades our whole being. A soul made for God, which finds itself in eternity cut off from God, is a complete misfit; to talk about a fish out of water would give no sort of idea what it means to be in eternity without the love of God. We are at war with ourselves, and our whole environment is at war with us. We can't imagine to ourselves, now, what the environment of a future life will be like; but we can be absolutely certain that, to the lost soul, that environment will be hostile.

Put it in this way—if a lost soul got into heaven by mistake, the music of heaven would seem to it like the most appalling series of discords. It carries the seeds of its own misery in itself. No need, I think, to talk of the pain of sense as if it were a punishment specially inflicted on the damned. Whatever there may be of sense experience in a future life must inevitably, to the lost soul, be a source of acute discomfort. Like a cracked bell, it must needs give out a false echo to every blow that is struck on it.

That's hell—complete disharmony with our surroundings, arising from and depending upon a complete disharmony within ourselves. A soul, by its own sins, violently pushed out of shape, warped into the wrong pattern, giving a false reaction, eternally, to every stimulus which a providentially ordered universe can offer it.

And now, if we miss hell, you and I—God grant we may—we shall nevertheless, it is to be feared, have a debt to pay off, for sins genuinely but insufficiently repented; a debt of suffering for those grave sins whose guilt has already been remitted in sacramental absolution, a debt of suffering for those venial sins which were not serious enough to cut us off from the friendship of God, but which were nevertheless an offence against him, and now claim retribution. That has got to happen in purgatory; how are we to think of purgatory?

Whatever the experience of purgatory will be like—and, as I say, we've awfully little apparatus for imagining what the experience of purgatory will be like—it will surely be accompanied by a sense of frustration. What do I mean by a sense of frustration? Why, when you take an enormous whang at a golf-ball, that is calculated to send it a couple of hundred yards down the fairway, and you top it and it just trickles a few yards; that's frustration. Effort on our part that achieves no proportionate result, because it is limited by circumstances outside ourselves; failure to express ourselves as we meant to. When you are particularly anxious to shine and shew to good advantage in somebody's company, and in spite of your anxiety or perhaps because of your anxiety you find yourself tongue-tied, or saying the opposite of what you meant to say; that is frustration. Wanting to hum a tune over to yourself and always, by a kind of fatality, getting one bar wrong; that is frustration. We are familiar with it at every turn of our lives; performance always comes a little short of promise; circumstances cramp our endeavours, and we do ourselves less than justice.

And here is a curious thing; when you go to bed and get to sleep, you would expect that this experience of frustration would be ruled out. In your dreams, you move in a world of pure fancy; no grim brick wall of fact to run your head up against; surely in your dreams all should go well, no effort should be misdirected, performance should go hand in hand with desire. And yet we know, don't we, that it's just the other way about; the sense of frustration pursues us, even in our dreams. You dream that you are in class, and the teacher is asking you a question, and for some reason it is very important, in your dream, that you should answer the question right. And you know the answer; it is fully present to your mind, but every time you open your mouth to give it, you find yourself singing a comic song, or something of that kind. That sense of frustration is the commonest symptom (I suppose) of nightmare.

There is a story of a man who was just in for his final exams at Oxford; and the night before his exam he dreamt that he died, and went to his judgment. He found himself queueing up in a dark hall, which looked curiously like the entrance hall of the examination schools; and an angel came and drew him to one side, where he found written up on the wall the Ten Commandments, as they used to be written up at the East end of Protestant churches. Only here he found written over the top of them: "Not more than five of these should be attempted." The sense of frustration which made him feel that he was going to do badly in his exam followed him into his dreams, and made him imagine that his whole life was one of frustrated effort.

Those of you who know your classics will know how the ancients pictured to themselves the future world—it was a dream life, a life of frustrated striving. The first thing Aeneas meets when he visits the underworld in the sixth book of the *Aeneid* is the souls of those unburied people who, because they had not received burial, could not get ferried across the river Styx; you remember that sad line, "Tendebantque manus ripae ulterioris amore"—they stretched out their hands in desire of the shore beyond. And when he comes across the Greek warriors who had fought against him at Troy, they try to raise their war-cry and rush at him, but their voice sticks in their throats—"Vox incassum frustratur hiantes"—their utterance eludes them as they open their mouths in vain. And when Aeneas tries to embrace his father Anchises, it is the same thing, "Thrice I tried to throw my arms around his neck, and thrice the shadowy form escaped my grasp". In the afterlife, the ancients thought, you cannot get where you want, you cannot say what you want to, you cannot satisfy, as you want to satisfy, the yearning of your affections.

And were the ancients altogether wrong? Or hadn't they really got onto the track of purgatory? Surely purgatory means that you want frightfully to get on, to reach the foreseen goal of heaven; want it much more badly than we ever do in this world, where we only know about heaven by hearsay, look forward to it by faith. And wanting it so badly, you find that you are frustrated of your desire; something keeps you back, keeps you back, from it. You can still pray; but your prayers, now, can do *you* no good; they are like the war-cry of the Greek heroes, they don't get you any further. The time for your prayers to do you any good is passed now; you should have said them while you were still alive. And you are wanting, desperately, to unite yourself with the love of God; because you have been given, at your Judgment, an awareness of God; and that awareness remains with you, urges you on, makes you impatient to achieve the enjoyment of it; but that enjoyment is not to be yours, not yet. Frustration, the sense of wanting to get somewhere, do something, enjoy something, and being unable to get anywhere, to do anything, to enjoy what you want to enjoy; years of that; that is purgatory, the inability to do, as yet, the one thing we have any faculty or any desire to do, that is, to enjoy God.

And heaven will be the contradiction of that; will mean

the unimpeded exercise of every faculty we have; eternal activity without restraint. Here again and with far more reason you may, if you will, concentrate your attention upon the accidental circumstances which help to make heaven what it is, without thinking directly about the essential part of heaven, which is the possession of God. There is happiness in heaven, there are pleasures in heaven. Not that we must fall into the mistake of the old heathens, who supposed that the next life is a mere continuation of this life —an error repeated by the modern spiritualists. We cannot suppose that the pleasures of the senses, eating and drinking and so on, persist in a world where we shall have no needs to satisfy.

Of course, we talk about people in heaven as being at rest. But heaven, clearly, does not mean hanging about and doing nothing for all eternity; there will be activity, the pleasurable exercise of our faculties—I always think that swimming gives you the nearest guess of what heaven will be like. I mean a really nice swim; the complete freedom of unlaborious movement, with no consciousness of obstacles. Heaven will not be dull; we shall always be doing the thing we want to do, and doing it perfectly. And again, heaven will mean rejoining those whom we have loved and lost; we shall enjoy exactly the company that is most congenial to us. And if you like to say, "That is enough for me; I am willing to serve for a life-time the God who engages my gratitude with such promises as these, without asking any further questions about what heaven will be like"— well, that will do; there is no necessity for your imagination to rise higher than that.

But you know, that is not the point of heaven. The point about heaven is the possession of God. And the best way to begin to understand what heaven will be like is this—

to cultivate, while you live on earth, as far as he gives you the grace to do it, the personal friendship of God; to experience, in that attempt, all the difficulties which our finite, earth-bound, sense-bound imagination necessarily encounters in pursuing the love of one who is invisible to us, who gives us no sensible sign of his nearness to us; to experience failure in our best efforts to serve him, weakness in our loyalty to him, fitfulness in our attention to him—in a word, to know what it is to love God without yet knowing what it is to be loved by God, and then, then when we attain heaven, what a revelation and what a consummation that will be! The aim we so long envisaged now at last within our grasp, the veil withdrawn, the intimacy realized, the betrothal turned into marriage.

Everybody will be satisfied in heaven; but everybody will be satisfied in proportion as he has wanted it; and those most of all, who wanted nothing in this world but God, and looked forward to their heaven only because God was there. Those faces will be happiest in heaven, those crowns the brightest; may he grant us, for all our unfaithfulness to him, some taste of that striving, some measure of that content.

21 *Personal Religion Again*

I HAVE been trying to direct your attention, all through this retreat, to the subject of personal religion; trying to suggest to you that we ought not to look upon our religion as a kind of formality which has got to be gone through, as a kind of duty, external altogether to ourselves, which we owe to a mysterious Power too distant to be conceived, too august to be mentioned without acute embarrassment, but rather as something close to ourselves, an intimate friendship with God. And accordingly I have insisted, for example, that the malice of sin and the peril of sin arise, really, from the fact that it is the betrayal of a supernatural friendship; that death is not a blind blow which strikes us from a distance, but an arrangement made personally for us by one who loves us better than we love ourselves, sees what is good for us far better than we can see it ourselves; that our heaven will be the enjoyment of God's presence, our punishment, if we miss heaven, banishment from his sight.

And while I have been doing that, I expect that some of you have been wanting to pull me up and say, "Yes, that's all very well, *but*. . . ." What a tiresome phrase that is, isn't it, when people say to you, "Yes, that is all very well, but. . . ." When you have really worked out the answer to a sum, or solved a problem in geometry, as it seems to you, with really remarkable skill, and then the teacher says,

"Yes, that is all very well, but. . . ." When you have shewn your father really convincing reasons why your pocket-money ought to be paid out on a more lavish scale, and he has listened to you so attentively that you really thought he was agreeing with you all the time, and then at the end he goes and spoils it all by saying, "Yes, that is all very well, but. . . ." And really there are very few arguments that we can produce, very few points of view we can put forward, which unkind critics cannot refute, or at all events disarm of their full effect, with the use of that forbidding formula, "Yes, that is all very well, but. . . ."

Now, in this particular instance, if you want to pick holes in the retreat I have given you, there is a quite simple way of doing it; and it is to say, "Yes, that is all very well, *but* isn't that more the Protestant point of view than the Catholic point of view about religion?"

After all, if you know anything about history, you will know that what the early Protestants were always insisting on was the idea that the soul ought to have direct access to its God; nobody and nothing was to be allowed to come between them. What was the use of having consecrated priests, to come between the soul and God? What was the use of having sacraments and ceremonies, to come between the soul and God? What was the use of having long formal prayers, to come between the soul and God? What was the use of honouring a whole heaven-full of saints, when devotion to them could only interrupt and interfere with the direct intimacy which ought to exist between the soul and God? That was their point of view; and if you had been following closely what I have been saying, which perhaps you haven't, and knew something about the real Protestant attitude, which perhaps you don't, that is the complaint you would be suggesting. You have been talking to us (you would say) as if we were a lot of Protestants; you have been making an appeal which it would be just as easy to make to Protestants as to Catholics. After all, if the whole of religion consists in personal intimacy with God, what is the point of going to Mass? What is the use of abstaining on Fridays? Why do we have to plough through a whole long catechism of 380 questions, if religion is nothing else than the love of God?

Well, you will have no difficulty in foreseeing what my answer is to that. I reply at once, "Yes, that is all very well, but. . . ." That is all very well, but just because Protestantism has got hold of a truth, that does not prove that Protestantism has got hold of the whole truth. Of course Protestantism has got hold of *a* truth; you did not imagine, did you, that it would have managed to survive all these centuries if there was nothing in it? To be sure, it has got hold of a bit of the truth; it sees that the important thing about religion is a personal relation with our Lord. But what it does not see is that if you really love our Lord the whole of the rest of the Catholic religion follows; you will want to believe in the Catholic faith and the Catholic Church because they are something closely connected with his own person. And that is what I want to talk about now; I want to shew you that if we really love God we shall also—having been brought up without any prejudices against it—want to love the Catholic religion.

You see, when all is said and done, friendship does not live on air. Two friends, if their friendship is to mean anything, must share a common world and live a common life. In the first place, you will always find that two friends will to some extent have common ideas. And again, they will have their common haunts, the scenes or the walks which they enjoy in common. And in the third place, they will not live entirely to themselves; they will have a common circle of acquaintances; the friends of one will be, some of them at least, friends of the other. And that is why the Catholic religion follows if we really love God. If we love God, we want to share his ideas, and therefore we are interested in everything which he has taught us by his revelation; we shall want to know and to believe the Catholic faith. If we love God, we shall want to share with him his favourite walks among men, and that means that we shall love the Catholic Church itself, which is the House of God, as St. Paul tells us. And if we love God we shall want to share his friendships; and that means we shall love the saints, who were distinguished by his friendship in life beyond the measure of their fellow-men.

First, then, I say that friendship commonly results in some sharing of ideas and of interests. It is extraordinary —I expect you must have noticed it for yourselves—how much we pick up our little tricks of manner from those with whom we live. Handwriting, for example; how common it is to see little flourishes of handwriting which one person has imitated, half deliberately, half unconsciously, from another!

Or again, in mere tricks of speech, how often you find that one friend will imitate another; not meaning to, but inevitably, as the result of seeing him often and sympathizing with him so closely. And all this half-conscious imitation is merely the index of a deeper truth—that two friends, whether they will or no, are constantly influencing each other's ideas. A. finds himself quite unexpectedly taking an interest in subjects he was never interested in before—why? Because he has caught the infection from B. And where the friendship is based, on one side, upon a strong intellectual admiration, it is extraordinary how much a friend's influence can educate and develop the tastes of a friend.

If we try to cultivate the friendship of God, there must be admiration on our side, and admiration, not least, of his infinite knowledge, his infinite wisdom. All the instruction that comes to us from him we value and we cherish precisely because it comes from him; we want to understand our Friend, and in order to do that we want to understand the ideas which he imparts to us.

Well, of course, strictly speaking, all knowledge whatever comes to us from God. And a scientist like Pasteur, investigating the mysterious secrets of nature about germs and inoculation and all that sort of thing, may, if he is a really religious man as Pasteur was, feel that all the researches which he makes into scientific truth bring him nearer, all the time, to understanding and loving his Divine Friend. But, for most of us, there is only one branch of learning which reminds us immediately of God and of God's friendship; and that is what we call religious knowledge. And I say this boldly; if you have really begun to love God, it will be quite impossible for you to lump religious knowledge with all other branches of education, and think of it as a tiresome drudgery, a tedious necessity, which you have to endure while you are at school but hope to escape from later on. To know what the Catholic religion teaches; to know how the Church defends her teaching against the criticisms of her enemies; to know what our religion stands for in history and in the world around us at the present moment—to know all that, according to the measure of intelligence which God gives us, is a natural desire of the Christian mind, a desire which will grow in all of us if we really love God.

I know that, when I say that, I am running counter to all your instincts, especially to that deep-seated instinct in you which tells you to distrust the highbrow. I am going to make it worse, by telling you that (as far as I have had the opportunity of observing) pupils at Catholic schools have a false tradition about Christian education; you think it is unimportant to know anything about your religion, so long as you practise your religion; and you are wrong. What will be the effect of it later on?

When you find yourself living among Protestants, as most of us have to do sooner or later, you will find that they want to know this or that about what the Catholic religion teaches, and, when they come and ask you, you will be forced to say, "Oh well, I never was much of a hand at Christian doctrine; you had better ask a priest." Or they will quote arguments against the Catholic religion which they have picked up somewhere, not as a rule very profound ones, but too profound for you, and you will be forced to reply, "Oh, I don't know; I have always taken that kind of thing on faith." An excellent thing that you should; but, you know, it does not impress people very much when they find that you should have so little to say about your religion or in defence of your religion. It makes them think that your religion is something strangely apart from yourself.

And in a sense they are right. It is possible, of course, to go on saying your prayers and making your Communions frequently and doing your best to keep God's commandments and do his will, and at the same time to be starving your intellectual nature by never *thinking* about religion at all. But that means a one-sided development of your nature, which may quite possibly prove a dangerous development. And it would not happen if you really loved God fearlessly and without reserve. You would not be afraid of thinking about your religion, you would not be shy of talking about your religion, if it really meant as much to you as an intimate friendship should mean, if it did really take its place in your life as a great spiritual romance.

Suppose you heard somebody talking about a friend of yours, even a casual friend, and he said, "It is a pity that he should be such a cad; it is a pity that he can never tell the truth; I should like him better if he were not such a conceited fool"; would you be content to say, "Oh, I don't know; I have never noticed that"? Would you be content to refer him to some third person, to give him a truer estimate of your friend's character? Of course you wouldn't; you would either want to argue with him or to knock him down. And yet here is an extraordinary thing; unbelievers will say the most outrageous things about Almighty God, that he is cruel, that he is unjust, that he is powerless to reward the good or punish the wicked; people will say the most outrageous things about the Catholic religion; that it is a tissue of superstition and fraud; that it fears the truth and despises all intellectual honesty; that it is demoralizing in its influence and fatal to the progress of the human race; and Catholics, sitting by and hearing this, can find no retort but—what? They can only say, "I never had much of a head for apologetics. To tell the truth, Christian doctrine always rather bored me." And then they go away thanking God that they at least have the gift of faith. I can't understand it; it absolutely beats me.

Your intellect, your tastes, must be in harmony with God's view of the world, or the friendship is in peril. And now for a different point; friendship generally means that the two friends have haunts in common. There are particular walks, or rooms, or scenes, which you associate with your friend, which are endeared to you by the association. And in particular, his own house, if he is grown up and has a house of his own. What an extraordinary thing it is, the way in which a house is often stamped with the personality of its owner! There is a book of Mr. Maurice Baring's, in which the

heroine after which it is named, Daphne Adeane, is dead
before the story opens, and yet she is really the heroine of
the story. Her husband has kept the house in which she
lived exactly as she left it; not a book must be disturbed,
not a vase of flowers but must be renewed, week after week,
just as she left it. And the result is that she is one of the most
influential characters in the story. Her power and her charm
linger in the deserted rooms, and impress themselves on the
living characters so as to have a decisive influence on the
plot. It will serve to illustrate my point, that human love or
friendship does overflow, as it were, into the material surroundings to which the friends are accustomed.

God's house is his Church. And by that I don't mean a
building like the building in which we are sitting; I don't
mean that it is necessary, because you love God, to take an
enormous interest in all the details of church furnishing. I
confess I have a certain distaste, and a certain distrust, for
people whose gossip is always of the sacristy; who, without
any professional reason for being interested in them, get
tremendously excited about the exact shape of an amice or
the exact number of indulgences which can be attached to a
rosary. I dare say that is my own fault, or the fault of my
upbringing; but for myself I always hope it is possible to love
God sincerely without knowing which end of the altar you
ought to start from when you light the candles—a point
which I can never get to stick in my head. No, I'm thinking
rather of the Church as an institution, with a history of her
own, with her wide diffusion throughout the world, and all
the problems which arise out of it, with all her complicated
network of charitable and spiritual activities. You will find
it will save a lot of trouble, and perhaps make you more
popular among your non-Catholic acquaintances, if you
grow up into the vague sort of Catholic; the sort of Catholic

who says, "Oh, I can't bear the Middle Ages, they're so stuffy", or "Are there really Catholics in Holland? I never knew that" or "I think we're in the Middlesborough diocese, but I'm never quite certain". It saves trouble, but it doesn't help things along. I don't want you to grow up into a Catholic bore, but I don't want you to grow up into a bored Catholic. It saves trouble, but it weakens the ties of your supernatural friendship.

And finally, if we would share a friendship we must share our friends. Each of us has his own world of acquaintance; and it is difficult for a friendship between two people to be lasting or to be natural unless their two worlds of acquaintance intersect. You cannot really understand your friend's character properly unless you know and appreciate something about the other people who enjoy his friendship; you do not know him unless you know the world he moves in. And if we are to enjoy God's friendship we must know his great friends, the saints, and appreciate something of their character, and establish, as far as it is possible for us, an intimacy with them too. If we think we love God, and yet have no love for the blessed saints in heaven, there is a danger that we are loving God in the wrong way, that we are misunderstanding his character. As St. John says, "He that loveth not his brother whom he hath seen, how can he love God whom he hath not seen?" If we are to recognize the goodness of God anywhere, we shall recognize it surely when we see it mirrored in the lives of the saints, human creatures like ourselves, and therefore easier for our human intelligences to understand.

And above all, of course, in our Blessed Lady. Instinctively, we look to her as our Mother, and each of us looks to her as *his* or *her* Mother, as being in a direct relationship to himself or herself, just as each of us can call God *my*

God. Not indeed that she is present, as God is present, everywhere at once; that is impossible for a creature. But we all have the instinct that she is accessible, at all times, to each of us, and interested in each of us. And indeed, how could it be otherwise? What good mother is there who does not make her son's interests her own, does not sympathize with all his ambitions and share all his anxieties? Our Lady is the best mother there ever was, and she is the mother of Jesus Christ, who cares individually for you and me; cares for me as if there were nobody else in the world but me, cares for you as if there were nobody else in the world but you. It is only natural, then, that our Blessed Lady should take a personal interest in you and me; are we not her Son's friends? Like a really good mother, she thinks of her Son's friends as her sons too.

With the other saints we are more inclined to pick and choose. One is the patron of our country, another of our school, we are named after another, another's character or career has impressed us when we read about it, and so on. And I think it is well that it should be so; I am not one of those who would try to impose one particular saint, generally the latest saint, on all my hearers, and make it almost a matter of faith to offer special devotion to this particular one. It is easy in that way to destroy the liberty of the spirit. I only say that your life as a Catholic will be definitely poorer, if there are not some names in the Calendar which thrill you more than others; your own name-saint, for example, or your school saints, or people whose lives you've read, or people you've picked up on the road-side as you go through life—they make some anniversary, or have helped you in some tight corner. They will help you to see God through their eyes; a kind of cross-reference which will deepen and enrich your friendship with him.

But I would just like to make one suggestion to you all in conclusion, and it is this; that you should read about, and think about, and follow with special reverence, the lives of saints who are your fellow-countrymen. For those who are English, there are the English martyrs—the men and women who laid down their lives for the faith during the persecutions of the sixteenth and seventeenth centuries. From St. Thomas More, who went with a joke to the scaffold, to Blessed John Kemble, who smoked a last pipe with the sheriff before he went out to execution, you will find them, I think, friends easy to get on with; here on earth and please God hereafter in heaven.

22 _End of Retreat_

RELIGION is a personal relationship between your soul and God, a loving service, a submissive love; in a sense, you may say it is that and nothing else. Let's suppose, for a moment, that you are wrecked on a desert island, all by yourself. Probably your first instinct, like Robinson Crusoe's, would be to build yourself a hut and light yourself a fire and make yourself comfortable in various ways which would have been quite impossible if you hadn't been a scout and known all about how to do that sort of thing. You would be fetching nails and bits of old soap boxes from the wreck to make yourself a hut with, and fishing for crabs with periwinkles, and setting traps for penguins with your shoe laces, and so on. And then, perhaps, as you were sitting down to a delicious fricassee of penguin, you'd suddenly say to yourself, "Gosh, I believe it's Friday; I ought to be eating that dressed crab after all." And then the day after the next would be Sunday; and you'd be wondering what you ought to do about that. Of course, you would stop building your hut, because that would have become servile work instead of being just fun. But you would be excused from going to Mass, not just this Sunday but every Sunday . . . and then it would occur to you that for the rest of your life, or at least until the first ship passed by and saw your sponge-bag on

the top of the pole, you had got to manage religion for yourself.

Well, that wouldn't be impossible; you'd be rather in the
position of the Fathers in the desert when you come to think
of it. Perhaps you would find that you couldn't remember
very many prayers by heart and would take to making up
prayers of your own and saying them. Then it might occur
to you that there wasn't much point in *saying* prayers when
there was nobody to say them with, you would content yourself with just *thinking* them. And then, perhaps, you would
reach a further stage.

I daresay you know the story of the old lady in the country who couldn't read and couldn't get about and lived miles
from anywhere; and when a kind visitor asked what she did
with herself all the time, she said, "Well, sometimes I sits
and thinks, and sometimes I just sits." I am not suggesting
that there is any form of prayer which could properly and
theologically be described as just sitting. But there is a form
of prayer, and some of the holiest people in the history of
our religion have practised it, which doesn't from the outside point of view look very much different; a kind of prayer
which not only does without words, but does, as far as possible, without any activity of the mind, any forming of pictures
or of considerations in the mind, which just throws itself
back on God and lets itself rest on God, and lets God dictate
both the subject and the manner of its praying, lets the Holy
Ghost, if I may put it in that way, do the praying for it and
in it. Cut off from books, from human companionship, from
events and incidents that mark off one day from another, you
might find yourself gradually growing into this way of prayer,
and you might reach a high degree of sanctity in the practice
of it.

Well, it's possible that God has, for some of you, a vocation to serve him in a special way by going out of the world and devoting yourselves to his service in religion. But if you are to remain in the world, and as long as you remain in the world, it is obvious that this personal friendship with God which is, I say, the essence of religion, will not be, for you, as simple an affair as when you sat and thought, or when you just sat, on your desert island. The world in which you live, the world which is at your elbow every day, will affect that friendship and set up cross-currents in it.

But, you know, the thing goes much further than that. When I tell you that you ought to read Catholic books, I'm not really asking you to do that so that you may have a pat answer to the next Protestant who heckles you. I'm thinking of your own faith, your own moral standards. The moment you leave school, and begin to rub shoulders with the world, it will begin to affect you; it has begun to affect you already, through the books you read, and the films you see, and the general culture which surrounds you. The world, I say; and I don't say it particularly because you live in a Protestant country, or because you live in an age which is intellectually fuddled.

In all ages, in all countries, the world acts as a solvent to Catholic piety; breathes an air in which Catholic piety languishes. Man's intellect always wants to approach things from the human side, from the side from which they can be known by man; shirks and burkes discussion of things from the side of reality, from the side which relates them to God. Man's art and literary genius is constantly concerned with man at his most human level, his passions, his craven fears, the rebellion of his will against the order in which he lives. All that breathes a poison, for which writers who care about the truth as it is in God have to provide an antidote; they must fight, they must react, but still more they must see things, they must record things, from that higher standpoint which is God's. You must, sometimes, give the lungs of your soul an airing on these heights, even if the atmosphere of it is more rare, is breathed with more effort, than the other. Or else, the miasma of the modern world will get you down, will weaken your resistance; you will be a prey to the germs of infidelity, to the infection of bad example.

And you will forget your Friend.

Knox, Ronald

AUTHOR

Retreat in Slow Motion

TITLE

Phone